P9-DBM-981

FITNESSGRAM®/ ACTIVITYGRAM®

Test Administration Manual

Updated Fourth Edition

Developed by:
The Cooper Institute
Dallas, Texas

Editors:
Marilu D. Meredith, EdD, Project Director
Gregory J. Welk, PhD, Scientific Director

Human Kinetics

ISBN-10: 0-7360-9992-1 (print)
ISBN-13: 978-0-7360-9992-9 (print)

Copyright © 2013, 2010, 2007, 2005, 2004, 1999, 1994 by The Cooper Institute

All rights reserved. Except for use in a review, the reproduction or utilization of this work in any form or by any electronic, mechanical, or other means, now known or hereafter invented, including xerography, photocopying, and recording, and in any information storage and retrieval system, is forbidden without the written permission of the publisher.

Notice: Educators who have purchased *FITNESSGRAM/ACTIVITYGRAM Test Administration Manual, Updated Fourth Edition,* have permission to reproduce materials on pages 90-107 and 110-117 for personal classroom use.

The right to install and run the *FITNESSGRAM/ACTIVITYGRAM Test Administration Manual DVD* and the *Combined PACER Tests With Cadences CD* as well as the right to broadcast the content within the educational classroom setting are extended to educators who have purchased this item. Any other use of this content, including download to another personal or commercial electronic system or device, or upload to any personal or commercial Web site accessible via the Internet, is expressly forbidden without written permission from the publisher.

The reproduction of other parts of this book or other uses of the DVD or CD are expressly forbidden by the above copyright notice. Persons or agencies who have not purchased *FITNESSGRAM/ACTIVITYGRAM Test Administration Manual, Updated Fourth Edition,* may not reproduce material or receive reproductions of this material in lieu of purchase.

The Web addresses cited in this text were current as of May 2010, unless otherwise noted.

Acquisitions Editors: Scott Wikgren and Kathy Read; **Managing Editor:** Laura Hambly; **Assistant Editor:** Derek Campbell; **Copyeditor:** Jan Feeney; **Permission Manager:** Dalene Reeder; **Graphic Designer:** Andrew Tietz; **Graphic Artist:** Denise Lowry; **Cover Designer:** Keith Blomberg; **Photographer (cover):** Neil Bernstein; **Photographer (interior):** © Human Kinetics, unless otherwise noted. Photos 6.1-6.7 by Jay Weesner; **Photo Asset Manager:** Laura Fitch; **Visual Production Assistant:** Joyce Brumfield; **Photo Production Manager:** Jason Allen; **Art Manager:** Kelly Hendren; **Associate Art Manager:** Alan L. Wilborn; **Illustrators:** Denise Lowry and Brian McElwain; **Printer:** United Graphics

Videos created through a project in the Department of Physical Education and Kinesiology at California State University, Bakersfield:

- **Kris Grappendorf**, Project Leader/Lecturer, Department of Physical Education and Kinesiology, California State University (Bakersfield), Bakersfield, CA

- **Dr. Anne Farrell**, Assistant Professor, Department of Physical Education, Health Education and Sports Studies, Canisius College, Buffalo, NY

- **Nicki Galante**, Physical Education Teacher, Warren Junior High School, Bakersfield, CA

- **Heidi Wegis**, Graduate Student, Department of Exercise and Sport Science, Oregon State University, Corvallis, OR

- Video production/editing, **John Lenko**, Kern County Superintendent of Schools

Students participating in the videos are from Warren Junior High School and Curran Middle School, Bakersfield, CA.

Printed in the United States of America   20   19   18   17   16

The paper in this book is certified under a sustainable forestry program.

Human Kinetics
Web site: www.HumanKinetics.com

United States: Human Kinetics, P.O. Box 5076, Champaign, IL 61825-5076
800-747-4457
email: info@hkusa.com

Canada: Human Kinetics, 475 Devonshire Road Unit 100, Windsor, ON N8Y 2L5
800-465-7301 (in Canada only)
email: info@hkcanada.com

Europe: Human Kinetics, 107 Bradford Road, Stanningley, Leeds LS28 6 AT, United Kingdom
+44 (0) 113 255 5665
email: hk@hkeurope.com

Australia: Human Kinetics, 57A Price Avenue, Lower Mitcham, South Australia 5062
08 8372 0999
e-mail: info@hkaustralia.com

New Zealand: Human Kinetics, P.O. Box 80, Mitcham Shopping Centre, South Australia 5062
0800 222 062
e-mail: info@hknewzealand.com

CONTENTS

Part III *ACTIVITYGRAM* Assessment Module

ACKNOWLEDGMENTS

The current version of *FITNESSGRAM/ACTIVITYGRAM* is the fifth revision of our youth fitness reporting system. During the last 10 years, many significant developments have occurred in the physical education field. In 1996, *Physical Activity and Health: A Report of the Surgeon General* was released. This provided strong documentation on the importance of physical activity for all segments of the population, especially children. In 1997, the Centers for Disease Control and Prevention released its report titled *Guidelines for School and Community Programs to Promote Lifelong Physical Activity Among Young People*. In 1998, the Council for Physical Education for Children (COPEC) released a statement on appropriate physical activity for children. Collectively, these developments provide physical educators and youth fitness promoters with considerable support and guidelines for promoting physical activity and fitness in children. The new version of *FITNESSGRAM/ACTIVITYGRAM* keeps pace with these developments and keeps you on the cutting edge of youth fitness promotion. The final product is the result of the cooperative efforts of many individuals.

Sincere appreciation is extended to the following people who serve on the *FITNESSGRAM/ACTIVITYGRAM* Advisory Board. Many dedicated hours have been spent in the continued development and refinement of the total program.

Kirk J. Cureton, PhD, University of Georgia

Scott Going, PhD, University of Arizona

Dolly Lambdin, PhD, University of Texas at Austin

Matt Mahar, EdD, East Carolina University

James R. Morrow, Jr., PhD, University of North Texas

Sharon A. Plowman, PhD, Northern Illinois University, retired

Stephen Pont, MD, MPH, FAAP, Dell Children's Medical Center

Judith Prochaska, PhD, MPH, University of California at San Francisco

Georgi Roberts, MS, Fort Worth ISD, Fort Worth, Texas

Weimo Zhu, PhD, University of Illinois at Urbana-Champaign

Marilu D. Meredith, EdD, The Cooper Institute, former program director

Don Disney, MS, MA, The Cooper Institute, director of youth initiatives

Catherine Vowell, MBA, The Cooper Institute, *FITNESSGRAM* director

Gregory J. Welk, PhD, Iowa State University, scientific director

Emeritus Members

Steven N. Blair, PED, MPH, University of South Carolina

Charles B. Corbin, PhD, Arizona State University, retired

Harold B. Falls, Jr., PhD, Southwest Missouri State University

Timothy G. Lohman, PhD, University of Arizona

Robert P. Pangrazi, PhD, Arizona State University, retired

Russell R. Pate, PhD, University of South Carolina

Margaret J. Safrit, PhD, American University

James F. Sallis, PhD, San Diego State University

Charles L. Sterling, EdD, The Cooper Institute, founder

HOW TO USE THIS MANUAL AND THE ENCLOSED DVD AND CD CLIPS

Part I of this manual provides important background information on *FITNESS-GRAM/ACTIVITYGRAM* and the role it plays within a complete physical education or physical activity program. Also included are testing guidelines and appropriate-use information.

Part II provides the *FITNESSGRAM* test administration protocols. This section is closely linked to the video clips on the enclosed DVD and provides details on how to administer each test.

Part III presents *ACTIVITYGRAM* administration information. This part of the manual explains how to use the *ACTIVITYGRAM* component and how to interpret the results.

Appendix A provides information on testing equipment. This section includes information about where to purchase and how to build special equipment for the physical fitness tests.

Appendix B provides the copy masters for the *FITNESSGRAM* and *ACTIVITYGRAM* programs. These can be copied straight from the manual to reproduce for students. Some of these masters are also located on the DVD so that colored copies can be created for students, used for posters, and so on.

Appendix C provides the health-related fitness tracking charts. These can be copied and used to track long-term progress for students.

Appendix D presents the software FAQs. This section includes the Internet addresses to the most commonly asked questions and detailed answers about the software, the *FITNESSGRAM* test administration, and *ACTIVITYGRAM* uses. If you have questions in these areas that are not addressed in the manual, please consult this information before calling the technical assistance line.

Appendix E provides the software user instructions. It includes step-by-step instructions and screen shots directly from the software to provide complete details for each action in the software. Combine the software instructions with the software training videos on the DVD. Follow the instructions as noted on these pages.

DVD Instructions

The enclosed DVD includes video clips for all of the text protocols and for the software as well as PDF files of forms and charts. The test protocol video clips demonstrate the proper way to implement each test and could also be used to demonstrate the proper technique to students.

You can view the video content either on a television set with a DVD player or on a computer with a DVD-ROM drive. The forms and charts can only be accessed through the DVD-ROM on your computer (see further instructions at the end of this section).

Test Administration and Software Training Video Clips

The DVD includes a main menu where you can select from the test protocol videos and the software training videos.

To use the DVD, place it in your DVD player or DVD-ROM drive. A title screen will welcome you to the program. Then the main menu will be displayed for the test protocols, software training videos, and the reproducible forms. Make your selection to view the videos or for instructions to access the forms. Note: The software training video clips can also be found on the **FITNESSGRAM** Web site (www.fitnessgram.net).

The following test protocol videos are available to view:

The PACER	Curl-up
One-mile run	Trunk lift
Walk test	Push-up
Triceps skinfold measurement	Modified pull-up
Calf skinfold measurement	Flexed arm hang
Abdominal skinfold measurement	Back-saver sit and reach
Body mass index	Shoulder stretch

The following forms are also available to print or view online using your DVD-ROM drive:

Overview of the New *FITNESSGRAM* Aerobic Capacity Standards

Overview of the New *FITNESSGRAM* Body Composition Standards

Standards for Healthy Fitness Zone—Boys

Standards for Healthy Fitness Zone—Girls

Get Fit Exercises

Get Fit Award

Fitness Contract

The PACER Individual Score Sheet A

PACER Test Individual Score Sheet B

The PACER Group Score Sheet

One-Mile Run Individual Score Sheet

Walk Test Individual Score Sheet

Body Composition Conversion Chart—Boys

Body Composition Conversion Chart—Girls

Personal Fitness Record (horizontal fold)

Personal Fitness Record (vertical fold)

ACTIVITYGRAM Assessment—Sample Log

ACTIVITYGRAM Assessment

Boy's Health-Related Fitness Tracking Charts

Girl's Health-Related Fitness Tracking Charts

ACTIVITYGRAM Physical Activity Log Booklet

8 Station Cards

To access the forms and charts from Windows®,

1. Insert the DVD into your DVD-ROM drive.
2. Access Windows® Explorer.
3. Right-click on the DVD-ROM drive icon, and select Open.
4. Click on the Worksheets folder, select the PDF file you want to view.

To access the form and charts on a Macintosh® computer,

1. Insert the DVD into your DVD-ROM drive.
2. Double-click on the "FITNESSGRAM" DVD icon on your desktop.
3. Select the PDF file you want to view.

Note: If your DVD viewing program is set to automatically launch, the video content will automatically run. You will need to close out of the DVD viewing program before accessing the PDF files.

You will need Adobe® Reader® to view the PDF files. If you do not already have Adobe Reader installed on your computer, go to www.adobe.com to download the free software.

Click on Human Kinetics on the main menu to access production credits and information on contacting Human Kinetics to order other products.

About the FITNESSGRAM Combined PACER Tests With Cadences CD

The FITNESSGRAM Combined PACER Tests With Cadences CD is a music CD and contains the following music versions for the PACER tests and the FITNESSGRAM test cadences:

- 20-meter PACER test with music
- 15-meter PACER test with music
- Cadence for the curl-up test
- Cadence for the push-up test

FITNESSGRAM and NFL Play 60

NFL Charities, the charitable foundation of the National Football League, partners with organizations to tackle childhood obesity through its NFL Play 60 program. Part of the NFL's long-standing commitment to health and fitness, NFL Play 60 challenges youth to become physically active for at least 60 minutes each day. Play 60 is also implemented locally as part of the NFL's in-school, after-school, and team-based programs.

The partnership between NFL Play 60 and The Cooper Institute's *FITNESSGRAM* includes implementing the *FITNESSGRAM* student test assessment in schools throughout the 32 NFL franchise communities. The assessment is part of a longitudinal study that tracks health-related fitness results and analyzes how best to intervene. The resulting data will be provided to local, state, and national policy makers.

www.Fitnessgram.net

The *FITNESSGRAM* Web site provides an excellent introduction for those who are unfamiliar with the program, but it does much more than that. The site also provides information for those who are considering a *FITNESSGRAM* software purchase as well as a wealth of resources to support *FITNESSGRAM* users. Here are some important features on the Web site:

- In-depth information about the research basis for *FITNESSGRAM* and the Healthy Fitness Zones: From Fitnessgram.net, click on the Reference Guide button
- Detailed system requirements and technical documents: Fitnessgram.net/support
- Frequently asked questions for parents: Fitnessgram.net/faqparents
- Sample reports: Fitnessgram.net/reports
- Information on training options: Fitnessgram.net/training
- Advocacy material for demonstrating the value of physical education and *FITNESSGRAM*: Fitnessgram. net/programoverview/advocacy
- Ready-made presentations for sharing *FITNESSGRAM* with decision-making personnel: Fitnessgram. net/presentations
- Support for current software customers: Fitnessgram.net/userinfo
- Contact information for your sales rep: Fitnessgram.net/contactus

PART I

INTRODUCTION TO FITNESSGRAM/ACTIVITYGRAM

FITNESSGRAM/ACTIVITYGRAM is a comprehensive health-related fitness and activity assessment and computerized reporting system. One of the unique features of the program is that it allows teachers to produce individualized reports for each student in a class. The reports provide feedback based on whether the child achieved the criterion-referenced standards for physical activity or fitness. The use of health-related criteria helps to minimize comparisons between children and to emphasize personal fitness for health rather than goals based on performance. There are two different assessment modules that can be used to help promote awareness about the importance of physical activity and physical fitness:

- *FITNESSGRAM* is a complete battery of health-related fitness items that are scored using criterion-referenced standards. These standards are age and gender specific and are established based on how fit children need to be for good health.
- *ACTIVITYGRAM* is an activity assessment tool that provides detailed information on a student's level of physical activity. Feedback is provided on the amount and type of activity that a child performs.

New information in this updated fourth edition of the *FITNESSGRAM/ACTIVITYGRAM Test Administration Manual* includes an announcement of the new criterion-referenced standards for aerobic capacity and body composition. The FITNESSGRAM Scientific Advisory Board has worked diligently during the past two years determining the appropriate changes for these standards. Specific information is available in chapters 5 and 6.

The *FITNESSGRAM* and *ACTIVITYGRAM* modules are linked to a powerful database system that allows data on individual students to be tracked and compiled over time. The computerized reporting system can also help teachers, schools, and districts track and document important student outcomes over time. The diverse components and features of *FITNESSGRAM* are designed to assist teachers in accomplishing the primary objective of youth fitness programs, which is to help students establish physical activity as a part of their daily lives. This manual provides documentation on the various assessment tools and instructions on how to get the most out of the software. *FITNESSGRAM* is described in Part II, *ACTIVITYGRAM* in Part III, and the software in Part IV.

The chapters in this part of the manual outline the mission and philosophy of the *FITNESSGRAM* program (chapter 1), describe principles of fitness education and assessment guidelines within physical education (chapter 2), and summarize guidelines needed to promote physical activity in children (chapter 3).

Presidential Youth Fitness Program

The Presidential Youth Fitness Program is a national program that includes fitness assessment, professional development, and recognition. Schools can adopt the program to assess, track, and award youth fitness and physical activity.

Forged from a first-of-its-kind partnership among some of the most influential and expert organizations in health and fitness education, assessment, and promotion, the Presidential Youth Fitness Program emphasizes the value of living a physically active and fit life—in school and beyond.

By adopting the Presidential Youth Fitness Program, schools gain access to a robust selection of resources that will help students engage in their own health and fitness:

A health-related assessment

Companion educational and motivational tools

Training materials

Awards

Launched in September 2012, the Presidential Youth Fitness Program (PYFP) adopted Fitnessgram® as the health-related assessment. For more information on the PYFP, please visit www.presidentialyouth fitnessprogram.org.

Need Additional Information?

Information on the validity and reliability of the tests and the rationale behind the establishment of the standards is available in the *FITNESSGRAM Reference Guide (FRG)*. The *Guide* has been developed in a question-and-answer format and is intended to address specific questions associated with use and interpretation of *ACTIVITYGRAM* and *FITNESSGRAM* assessments. The information in the *Guide* may be of interest to some parents who want more information about fitness. To facilitate its use, it is available on the Internet from the *FITNESSGRAM* Web site. Go to www.fitnessgram. net and click on Reference Guide.

CHAPTER 1

MISSION, GOALS, AND PHILOSOPHY OF FITNESSGRAM/ACTIVITYGRAM

Mission

The principal mission of the *FITNESSGRAM/ACTIVI-TYGRAM* program is to promote lifelong physical activity among youth. The program endorses a long-term view of physical education in which the promotion of lifelong habits of physical activity is the primary goal. Developing fitness and improving skills are important in physical education, but these objectives should be framed within a broader goal aimed at providing children with the knowledge, attitudes, and skills to be active for a lifetime.

Goals and Program Components

The specific program goals of *FITNESSGRAM/ ACTIVITYGRAM* are to promote enjoyable regular physical activity and to provide comprehensive physical fitness and activity assessments and reporting programs for children and youth. The program seeks to develop affective, cognitive, and behavioral components related to participation in regular physical activity in all children and youth, regardless of gender, age, disability, or any other factor. We believe that regular physical activity contributes to good health, function, and well-being and is important throughout a person's lifetime. The use of both *ACTIVITYGRAM* and *FITNESSGRAM* as part of a quality physical education program can help in accomplishing these goals. The descriptions that follow provide additional information on these components of the *FITNESSGRAM* program.

FITNESSGRAM

FITNESSGRAM is a comprehensive fitness assessment battery for youth. It includes a variety of health-related physical fitness tests designed to assess cardiovascular fitness, muscle strength, muscular endurance, flexibility, and body composition.

Criterion-referenced standards associated with good health have been established for children and youth for each of the health-related fitness components.

FITNESSGRAM is also a report card that summarizes the child's performance on each component of health-related fitness. *FITNESSGRAM* can be used by students, teachers, and parents. Students can use *FITNESSGRAM* in planning their personal fitness programs; teachers can use it to determine student needs and help guide students in program planning; and parents can use it to help them understand their child's needs and help the child plan a program of physical activity.

FITNESSGRAM uses a comprehensive database structure to allow fitness records to be tracked over time and detailed reporting tools that can be used to summarize class, school, and district outcomes. The database can help teachers document and organize information on student outcomes.

ACTIVITYGRAM

ACTIVITYGRAM is a detailed (three-day) assessment of physical activity. The assessment is designed to provide students with personal information about their general levels of physical activity and to help individuals learn strategies to be physically active both in and outside of school. Reports provide information on the amount of activity children perform, a graphical display of their activity patterns, and an indication of the different types of activities that they perform. The feedback can help students learn how to set up programs to increase participation in moderate and vigorous physical activity, in strength and flexibility activities, and in lifestyle activities. *ACTIVITYGRAM* uses the physical activity pyramid as a basis for analyzing personal activity patterns.

Program Philosophy (HELP)

The mission, goals, and program components of *FITNESSGRAM* are embedded within a unifying philosophy that guides program development and components of the software. We refer to this philosophy as the "HELP Philosophy" (see figure 1.1). HELP is an acronym specifying that *"**h**ealth is available to **e**veryone for a **l**ifetime—and it's **p**ersonal."* The following paragraphs provide descriptions for each of the components.

Health

Physical activity provides important health benefits and can enhance the quality of life for both children and adults. Improvements in different dimensions of health-related physical fitness (aerobic capacity; body composition; and muscular strength, endurance, and flexibility) result from regular participation in physical activity. The criterion-referenced standards in *FITNESSGRAM* are based on the level of fitness needed for good health. Similar activity guidelines in *ACTIVITYGRAM* are based on how active children should be for optimal health.

Everyone

All children can be successful in *FITNESSGRAM*. While some physical fitness programs emphasize the attainment of high levels of performance on components of fitness, we believe that extremely high levels of physical fitness (while admirable) are not necessary to accomplish objectives associated with good health and improved function. With reasonable amounts of physical activity, all children can receive sufficient health benefits. In a free society, individuals choose what they want to emphasize and where they want to strive for excellence. Some students will decide to make such an effort in the sciences, music, art, or drama; others (for example, athletes) will give high priority to physical activity and fitness. We recognize this as proper, and we view *FITNESSGRAM/ACTIVITYGRAM* as a way to help all children and youth achieve a level of activity and fitness associated with good health, growth, and function.

Lifetime

Physical activity must be maintained over time in order to continue to provide benefits. A major determinant of lifetime physical activity is gaining confidence in skills and behaviors associated with physical activity (self-efficacy). Assessments should be aimed at enhancing self-efficacy. Assessment activities that improve perceptions of competence are encouraged, and those that undermine self-efficacy are discouraged. Accordingly, self-comparisons of results over time or self-comparisons to health standards are encouraged. Interstudent comparisons of private, personal self-assessment data are discouraged.

Personal

Because fitness is personal, it is important that privacy of results be a priority when one is using *ACTIVITYGRAM* and *FITNESSGRAM*. The data collected during the assessments should be con-

H	**H** stands for **HEALTH** and health-related fitness. The primary goal of the program is to promote regular physical activity among all youth. Of particular importance is promoting activity patterns that lead to reduced health risk and improved health-related physical fitness.
E	**E** stands for **EVERYONE**. The *FITNESSGRAM/ACTIVITYGRAM* program is designed for all people regardless of physical ability. Used together, *FITNESSGRAM* and *ACTIVITYGRAM* assessments are designed to help ALL youth find some form of activity that they can do for a lifetime. Too often activity programs are perceived to be only for those who are "good" rather than for all people. Physical activity and fitness are for everyone regardless of age, gender, or ability.
L	**L** stands for **LIFETIME**. *FITNESSGRAM* and *ACTIVITYGRAM* have as a goal helping young people to be active now, but a long-term goal is to help them learn to do activities that they will continue to perform throughout their lives.
P	**P** stands for **PERSONAL**. No two people are exactly the same. No two people enjoy the exact same activities. *FITNESSGRAM* and *ACTIVITYGRAM* are designed to personalize physical activity to meet **PERSONAL** or individual needs.

FIGURE 1.1   The HELP philosophy of *ACTIVITYGRAM* and *FITNESSGRAM*.

Reprinted, by permission, from C.B. Corbin and R. Lindsey, 2005, *Fitness for Life*, 5th ed. (Champaign, IL: Human Kinetics).

sidered personal information, and appropriate care should be taken when administering the tests and discussing the results. Ensuring confidentiality with the assessments will help individuals focus on their personal needs and be less concerned about comparisons with others.

CHAPTER 2

FITNESS EDUCATION AND ASSESSMENT GUIDELINES

The ultimate (long-term) objective of a physical education program is to teach students the physical and behavioral skills they need to be active for life. This objective should be viewed as the culmination or final outcome of a well-executed K-12 curriculum. To reach this objective, most experts recommend the use of a hierarchical curriculum that builds with each passing year. An effective fitness education program must help to build both the physical and behavioral skills needed to be physically active throughout life.

The recommended progression of *physical skills* in physical education can be likened to the progressions used to teach and reinforce reading. Just as students first learn basic words and basic sentences, they must also learn to first master basic physical skills. As children develop, they need opportunities to practice and apply skills in games. This is analogous to the need for developing readers to start reading books. With further development, students can learn ways to enhance their skills and apply them to the sports and activities that most interest them. This is similar to what happens when students eventually learn to read

different types of materials to learn about subjects of interest. In physical development (just as in reading development), the progression of material must be systematic and must build with each passing year. The conceptual diagram in figure 2.1 highlights the recommended objectives at each level of development. In the elementary years, emphasis should be on providing opportunities for children to experience and enjoy a variety of activities. Learning and practicing physical skills are critical at this stage since these activities help build self-efficacy and perceptions of competence. A good repertoire of skills will also make it easier for children to learn sports and lifetime activities that they can perform as they get older. At the middle school level, focus should shift to skill instruction so children can master specific movement skills. Care should be taken to minimize experiences of failure, since long-term attitudes may begin to form at these ages. In high school, students should be given more choice about the activities that they perform. The key concept in this diagram is that the scope of activities and nature of instruction broaden through elementary

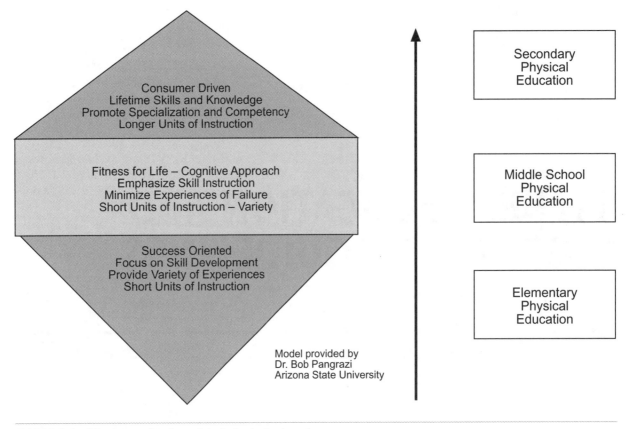

FIGURE 2.1   The hierarchical model of physical education.

Reprinted, by permission, from Dr. Bob Pangrazi, Department of Exercise Science & Physical Education, Arizona State University.

school and into middle school and then taper off into high school. Although each teacher may be involved with only a few grade levels, all teachers need to understand the progression of experiences recommended in physical education.

Behavioral skills are also needed to increase the chance that children will be active throughout their lives. Students ultimately need to learn to self-assess their fitness levels, interpret assessment results, plan personal programs, and motivate themselves to remain active on their own. Instruction on behavioral skills requires a similar progression over the K-12 curriculum. The fitness and activity assessments in the *FITNESSGRAM/ ACTIVITYGRAM* program provide tools that teachers can use to teach these concepts, but the purpose of the assessments and the depth of coverage should be matched to the interests and abilities of the children. The following sections highlight the recommended uses and applications of *FITNESSGRAM/ACTIVITYGRAM* assessments in the physical education curriculum.

Assessment Options for Fitness Education

FITNESSGRAM/ACTIVITYGRAM is designed to help evaluate and educate youth about levels of physical activity and their physical fitness. This information can be used in different ways depending on the philosophy of the district, school, and individual teachers. Various assessment procedures are possible depending on the primary objective of the program. The following sections describe the primary assessment options.

Self-Testing and Self-Assessment

Self-testing refers to personal assessments made by individual students of their own fitness and activity levels. Students are taught to give the tests to themselves or to each other and to interpret their own test results. Once students become accomplished in self-testing they can repeat testing periodically to assess personal improvement.

Teaching self-testing is an important objective in physical education since it provides the necessary tools and experience for students to learn how to test themselves and plan personal programs throughout life. It takes a considerable amount of practice to self-test effectively, so multiple opportunities to practice are necessary. Self-testing results are considered personal. For this reason, student information may be kept personal if a student desires. Personal *FITNESSGRAM* reports may still be printed, but students should decide if they want to share their personal information. Test results for beginning self-testers are not particularly accurate, and this point should be emphasized to both students and parents (if results are shared).

Individualized Testing

Individualized testing is aimed at providing students with accurate indicators of their fitness and physical activity levels. Students in physical education should learn whether or not they have sufficient amounts of fitness for good health and whether they are performing sufficient amounts of activity. Both *FITNESSGRAM* and *ACTIVITYGRAM* use criterion-referenced standards that are based on appropriate health-related criteria. The software and printed reports provide prescriptive feedback depending on whether the child attained the Healthy Fitness Zone for the various dimensions of fitness or the total amounts of activity. Students who fail to reach the Healthy Fitness Zone receive the feedback needed to develop a program of improvement. Students who reach the Healthy Fitness Zone receive information on how to maintain their fitness or activity levels.

In some situations, teachers may elect to have students stop the test when they have achieved a score equal to the upper limit of the Healthy Fitness Zone. Stopping the test performance in this manner can reduce required testing time. It may also reduce the possibility of embarrassment and avoid creating a threatening environment caused by assessments for students who are less capable or fit. With use of this approach, parents should be informed about the process so they understand that the performance reported on *FITNESSGRAM* does not necessarily represent a maximal effort.

A main goal of the *FITNESSGRAM/ACTIVITYGRAM* program is to help keep parents informed about their child's level of health-related fitness and activity habits. By sending the personalized report home to parents, the teacher can communicate individualized results to the parents. If reports are sent home, it is important that parents be instructed in how to interpret test results. Ways to do this are through cover memos or direct interaction at parent-teacher conferences. The goal of this type of communication is to enhance parental involvement in the promotion of physical activity (see chapter 3). Parents should be encouraged to use the personalized messages to help students plan personal programs of activity that are suited to each child's individual needs. If parental feedback is used, our recommendation is that students be informed so that they are aware that the results will be shared with their families.

Results from *FITNESSGRAM/ACTIVITYGRAM* can be tracked over time on charts to provide a personalized fitness "portfolio." Student results may be plotted on a regular basis to show whether children retain their fitness status over time. The goal is to help all youth meet or exceed criterion-referenced standards on all parts of fitness over time. When dramatic changes in personal performance occur, tracking will help the student, the teacher, and the parent identify reasons for changes.

Institutional Testing

Institutional testing refers to assessments conducted to help teachers determine the levels of activity, fitness, or both activity and fitness in groups of students. It is referred to as "institutional" testing since it may be required by the school or district as a way to document and track student outcomes. This type of testing requires a more structured and formalized approach than either self-testing or individualized testing since it is important to ensure that the tests are administered consistently across classes and over time. It is recommended that teachers closely adhere to the established *FITNESSGRAM* test protocols to improve the reliability and validity of the results. Because the assessments may require feedback and judgment to determine number of repetitions, additional testers or assistants may be needed to help administer the tests and document results. The added structure takes additional time but is necessary if the results are to provide meaningful information.

Because this type of testing may take time away from other portions of the curriculum, schools and districts should consider the educational ramifications associated with regular institutional fitness testing. For overall monitoring, this type of testing need only be done periodically (for example every third year), similar to the way many schools conduct educational assessments using standardized tests such as the Iowa Test of Basic Skills (ITBS). If annual institutional testing is to be done, the recommendation is that it always be done at the same time of the year (beginning or end). Care should be taken in the interpretation of data obtained from this type of testing. As pointed out in this chapter, results on fitness testing should not be used for determining student grades, long-term student achievement, or teacher success. As noted in the *FITNESSGRAM Reference Guide,* fitness tests cannot be regarded as good indicators of student achievement because there are too many factors other than physical activity that influence fitness.

Personal Best Testing

Personal best testing refers to special situations in which some students may strive to achieve their personal best scores on specific fitness tests. Because all children and youth may not be interested in high performance results, this type of testing is not recommended for all students. This type of testing is best done before or after school on a voluntary basis. The *FITNESSGRAM* philosophy focuses on good health, and high levels of fitness are not necessary for good health. Some youth, however, may be interested in achieving high levels of fitness to meet performance goals, and teachers may wish to provide the opportunity for such personal best testing.

Effective and Appropriate Use of ACTIVITYGRAM and FITNESSGRAM Assessments in Physical Education

This section outlines appropriate uses for *FITNESS-GRAM* and *ACTIVITYGRAM* and also identifies ways in which these programs should *not* be used. We then present recommendations for use of the *FITNESSGRAM* software in program evaluation.

Appropriate Uses for ACTIVITYGRAM

ACTIVITYGRAM was designed to help youth learn to self-monitor their personal physical activity patterns. Learning to self-monitor physical activity helps students to see "how active they really are" and helps them in setting goals for planning life-time activity programs. Self-monitoring, goal setting, and program planning are considered "self-management skills," and learning self-management skills is considered essential to lifetime physical activity adherence (Dale, Corbin, and Cuddihy, 1998; Dale and Corbin, 2000).

The *ACTIVITYGRAM* assessment requires the ability to recall bouts of physical activity over the past few days and to categorize activity by type, intensity, and duration. While young children can recall different activities they perform, concepts of time and perceptions of intensity are not well established in younger children. Therefore, *ACTIVI-TYGRAM* is not intended for children under the age of 10. Older elementary grade students may also have difficulty with the cognitive aspects of recall, so emphasis should be on the process of completing the assessments.

ACTIVITYGRAM can be used for institutional testing if standardized protocols are used for collecting the information, but proper consideration should be given to interpreting the accuracy of self-reported information. The box below summarizes the appropriate uses of *ACTIVITYGRAM* in physical education.

Appropriate Uses for FITNESSGRAM

The major purpose of *FITNESSGRAM* is to provide the student, teacher, and parents with personal information regarding the student's current level of fitness. The information regarding fitness status

---

Appropriate Uses for *ACTIVITYGRAM*

- Personal testing to help students assess their current level of activity

- Institutional testing to allow teachers to view group data (for curriculum development)

- Teaching students about different types and intensities of activity and the health benefits of being physically active

- Helping students self-monitor physical activity over time (in portfolios, for example)

- Documenting that *ACTIVITYGRAM* is being administered in schools and that student self-assessments are being tracked over time

can then be used as the basis for designing personal, individualized programs of fitness development. As previously described, the emphasis in physical education should vary across the K-12 curriculum to address higher-order learning objectives and take into account developmental needs of students. Similarly, the use of fitness testing should also be variable across the K-12 curriculum. At young ages, physical activity is not strongly linked to physical fitness. Therefore, an emphasis on structured fitness testing through the *FITNESSGRAM* battery is not recommended for children in grades K-3. The goal at this age should be to expose children to the different test items and help them learn about the various parts of physical fitness. Self-testing is recommended as the primary means to teach children about these assessments.

Older elementary students are able to understand the different dimensions of fitness and may appreciate the feedback from the assessments. Formal institutional testing is not necessarily recommended, but structured individual testing can provide meaningful information for children and parents as well as teachers. In middle school and high school the curriculum can include self-testing as well as individual and periodic institutionalized testing. Emphasis should change across different years so that students do not come to dread the repeated use of testing every year.

Some teachers feel that tests at the beginning of the year and again at the end of the year are good indicators of student achievement. While this type of testing may be used, the results must be interpreted with caution. First, students will improve whether they are doing activity or not, just because they are getting older. For this reason, incorrect messages may be conveyed. Second, students learn over a period of time to "be bad" on initial tests and "get good" on later tests if grades are based on improvement. The box below summarizes the appropriate uses of *FITNESSGRAM* in physical education.

Inappropriate Uses for ACTIVITYGRAM and FITNESSGRAM

1. **Student scores on *ACTIVITYGRAM* and *FITNESSGRAM* should NOT be used to evaluate individual students in physical education (e.g., grading or state standards testing).** Students are different in terms of interests and ability. Grading students on their fitness performance may be holding them accountable for accomplishments beyond their control. Posting the results for other students to see can create an embarrassing situation that does little to foster positive attitudes toward activity.

2. **Student scores on *ACTIVITYGRAM* and *FITNESSGRAM* should NOT be used to evaluate teacher effectiveness (e.g., teacher evaluations).** Teachers can be effective at teaching youngsters how to develop and maintain physical fitness and still have students who do not perform well on fitness tests. Often, physical education teachers who emphasize only fitness activities may be short-changing their students in other areas such as skill development, social skills, and positive attitudes toward physical activity.

3. **Student scores on *ACTIVITYGRAM* and *FITNESSGRAM* should NOT be used to evaluate overall physical education quality (e.g., physical education program assessment).** Promoting physical fitness is only one part of a quality physical education program. Teaching physical skills, cooperative skills, and health maintenance skills are equally important objectives for promoting lifelong physical activity.

Appropriate Uses for *FITNESSGRAM*

- Personal testing to help students evaluate their level of health-related fitness

- Institutional testing to allow teachers to view group data (for curriculum development)

- "Personal best" testing to allow individual students to privately determine performance levels

- Teaching students about criterion-referenced health standards and what types of activity are needed to reach them

- Helping students track fitness results over time (in portfolios, for example)

- Documenting that *FITNESSGRAM* is being administered in schools and that student self-assessments are being tracked over time is appropriate

Recommended Approaches for Program Evaluation

For better or for worse, there is an increasing emphasis on standardized testing in schools—and physical education is no exception. Education programs at all levels are increasingly being asked to document that they are monitoring and achieving stated learning objectives. Therefore, there is a need to develop a systematic approach to document important outcomes in physical education. There currently is no established national standard, and the standards and criteria vary considerably across states. While teachers may not have complete autonomy to prepare their own evaluation plans, it is important for them to be aware of the issues and be able to defend criteria that are appropriate to use in evaluating their program.

A common approach is establishing criteria to define the percentage of the student body that should achieve the Healthy Fitness Zone or above. Establishment of appropriate criteria is difficult since the percentage of students achieving the Healthy Fitness Zone varies. The assumption in some cases is that if the curriculum or program is adequate, then most students should be able to achieve these institutional goals. In this model, teachers reporting values below the stated goals may be asked to make systematic changes in their program to increase the percentage of students achieving the goals. As described previously, student fitness outcomes are not completely within a teacher's control. Teachers forced to comply with this type of evaluation system may be forced to "teach to the test" and emphasize only fitness attainment at the expense of other educational outcomes. Student attainment of fitness outcomes does not provide a good indication of program quality and other indicators should be considered for evaluation.

Some districts are interested in tracking trends over time. Changes in passing rates over time can provide useful information for curriculum planning. Program coordinators can compare fitness and activity levels of similarly aged children to evaluate the utility of new lessons or initiatives. This type of documentation can help to provide some accountability for the overall program. The *FITNESSGRAM* software provides a number of useful tracking and report functions to facilitate documentation of group results. Information on these report functions can be found in the software section of this manual. Additional information on program evaluation guidelines can be found in the *FITNESSGRAM Reference Guide.* Schools and districts are encouraged to carefully consider the relative merits of different evaluation criteria. Emphasis should be placed on quality-improvement approaches that systematically seek to improve on the overall programs.

Need Additional Information?

A copy of the *FITNESSGRAM* position on appropriate and inappropriate uses of fitness and activity assessment can be found within the *FITNESSGRAM Reference Guide* and may be downloaded at www.fitnessgram.net.

The Assessment Process Step by Step

A generic assessment process is provided below to facilitate basic instruction on fitness. The assessment process consists of eight steps, beginning with instruction about activity and fitness concepts and ending with revision and readjustment of the physical activity program.

Step One: Instruction About Activity and Fitness Concepts

Students should be instructed in basic concepts of fitness development and maintenance. Concepts should include the following:

- Importance of regular exercise for health and the prevention of degenerative diseases
- Description of each area of fitness and its importance to health
- Methods to use in developing each area of fitness

Step Two: Student Participation in Conditioning Activities

If fitness testing is being conducted, students should be preconditioned for testing to maximize safety. The Get Fit Conditioning Program provided in appendix B on page 90 may be used for this purpose. Do some of these activities in class; assign others for completion during the student's leisure time.

Step Three: Instruction on Test Items

Include the following topics when teaching each test item:

- Why it is important for health
- What it measures
- How to administer it
- Practice sessions

Step Four: Assessment of Fitness Levels

If possible, allow students to test one another or have a team of parents assist in conducting the assessments. Also, teach students to conduct self-assessments.

Step Five: Planning the Fitness Program and Setting Goals

After completing the fitness tests, use the results to help each student set goals and plan his or her personal fitness program. Activity goals can emphasize areas in which the student has the greatest needs.

Be sure to include the following activities:

- Inform students and parents of results with the *FITNESSGRAM* or the *ACTIVITYGRAM* reports.
- Teach students how to interpret their results.
- Assist students in setting process goals for an exercise program that will improve or maintain their fitness levels or their activity levels (see appendix B for goal-setting form).
- Evaluate group performance.

Step Six: Promoting and Tracking Physical Activity

The teacher or fitness leader should make every effort to motivate students to establish regular physical activity habits and to recognize students for success in their efforts. The Activity Log module may be useful to help students learn how to monitor their physical activity levels. Periodic use of the *ACTIVITYGRAM* assessment can provide a more comprehensive evaluation of overall activity patterns. The use of these tools as well as the use of the Presidential Active Lifestyle Award as a behavioral incentive can help to promote physical activity in students.

Allow time during physical education for students to work toward their goals. You should also expect them to spend some of their leisure time participating in fun activities that will help them achieve their goals. The critical consideration is that students should have FUN while participating in physical activity.

Step Seven: Reassessment

Periodic reassessment apprises students of how they are changing and reinforces for them the practice of "sticking with it." When you report their results, show the progress of individuals using individualized reports and of the group using a group statistical report. Both reports may be used to show change in scores from the previous test period, and this can help denote progress. Recognition for achieving goals is a vital part of establishing behavior patterns.

Step Eight: Revision

Reassessment yields new information so that you can revise or refine goals. In a physical education setting it is important to provide individualized feedback to students so they know what areas they should work on the most. However, a major instructional goal should be to teach students how to evaluate their own results and make their own personal goals.

Curriculum With Links to FITNESSGRAM

While a number of different physical education curricula are available to teach principles of fitness education, there are some that have direct conceptual and philosophical links with the *FITNESSGRAM* program. This section describes Physical Best and Fitness for Life as two examples.

Physical Best

Physical Best is a companion product to *FITNESSGRAM/ACTIVITYGRAM*. Developed by the American Alliance for Health, Physical Education, Recreation and Dance (AAHPERD), *Physical Best* is a complete educational program for teaching health-related fitness concepts. Learning activities are included for the areas of health-related fitness: aerobic capacity; body composition; and muscle strength, endurance, and flexibility. The curriculum covers all health-related fitness components and has components that can be used to promote parent and community involvement. Physical Best is unique as a physical education curriculum in a number of ways.

- Physical Best is *inclusive* in that it provides developmentally appropriate activities for different ages and abilities.

- Physical Best is *personal* in the way that it focuses on each child's individual preferences and capabilities.
- Physical Best is criterion referenced in its use of established health guidelines. Personal improvement is emphasized rather than unrealistic performance-based standards.
- Physical Best teaches cognitive knowledge *through* physical activity.
- Physical Best is created by teachers for teachers:
  - The program is a result of the work of practitioners who have used the activities and teaching methods in the classroom.
  - The ongoing development of the program is guided by a steering committee of AAHPERD members.

All of these characteristics combined with *FITNESSGRAM/ACTIVITYGRAM* form a comprehensive program that provides one-stop shopping for physical activity, nutrition education, and assessment in fitness education. Physical Best is also linked to national education standards (NASPE, AAHE, NDA), provides accountability for educators by tying to national standards, and is a K-12 program with resources appropriate to every grade level.

Fitness for Life

Fitness for Life is a comprehensive K-12 program that helps students take responsibility for their own activity, fitness, and health and prepares them to be physically active and healthy throughout their adult lives. This standards-based program is carefully articulated and follows a pedagogically sound scope and sequence to enhance student learning and progress.

The *Fitness for Life* program includes three sets of coordinated resources:

1. A K-6 nutrition, physical activity, and wellness program
2. A personal fitness text for middle school students
3. The nation's first personal fitness textbook for teens, now in its updated fifth edition

Fitness for Life is designed to be integrated with other physical education activities to create a high-quality, comprehensive physical education program. *Fitness for Life* is also fully integrated with Physical Best and *FITNESSGRAM*, sharing the same HELP philosophy.

The materials contain specific guidelines to assist students in learning how to evaluate and interpret their own fitness scores (based on *FITNESSGRAM* assessments) and how to build behavioral skills needed for lifetime fitness. The *Fitness for Life* program is an ideal way to achieve higher-level learning outcomes in elementary and secondary physical education.

Need Additional Information?

To order *Physical Best* and *Fitness for Life* materials, call Human Kinetics at 800-747-4457 ext 5555, or order online at www.HumanKinetics.com.

CHAPTER 3

PROMOTING PHYSICAL ACTIVITY

The benefits of an active lifestyle have been known for a long time, but the importance of physical activity has received greater attention in recent years. Much of the attention is due to the highly publicized epidemic of obesity that is affecting the United States and most developed countries. Trends compiled over the past 10 to 15 years indicate that the prevalence of obesity has increased over 50% since 1990. The trends are consistent across all age groups, both genders, and all races and ethnicities. There is considerable concern about the increasing prevalence of overweight in children as it is well established that overweight and obesity track throughout the lifespan.

The purpose of this chapter is to describe the rationale for an emphasis on promoting physical activity within physical education. The Youth Physical Activity Promotion Model is used to illustrate different ways in which teachers can help promote children's physical activity behavior. The last section of the chapter presents information on the value and utility of recognition systems in rewarding and promoting physical activity behavior.

The Importance of Promoting Physical Activity in Physical Education

Over the years, the goals and objectives of physical education have evolved to fit the prevailing public health views regarding the contributions of physical activity and fitness to health and well-being. The recent shift in public health policy toward the importance of regular physical activity has led to changes in the way physical education is viewed. While physical fitness is still considered an important goal for physical education, the general consensus is that it is more important to focus on promoting the process (behavior) of physical activity than the product (outcome) of fitness. A primary reason is that physical activity has the potential to track into adulthood. Fitness, on the other hand, is transient and will be maintained only if the child remains physically active. Thus, the key role of physical education is to promote lifetime physical activity.

Communicating the importance of physical activity to children may be difficult if fitness testing is used as the sole form of evaluation in the physical education curriculum. For example, if a child scores well on fitness testing without being active, he or she may believe that it is not necessary to be active on a regular basis. Conversely, children who are active but who score poorly on fitness tests may lose confidence and develop negative attitudes toward physical activity. To promote lifetime physical activity, it is important to provide instruction and reinforcement directly on the behavior rather than on the intended outcome. The incorporation of activity messages into the *FITNESSGRAM* module and the development of the behaviorally based *ACTIVITYGRAM* module (and the upcoming release of an Activity Log) can help to facilitate this shift in conceptual focus within physical education. While children can learn about the relationships between physical activity and physical fitness through the interactive *FITNESSGRAM* software, it is incumbent upon the physical education teacher to help promote lifetime physical activity among the children.

Physical Activity Guidelines

The current youth physical activity guidelines (as presented in the COPEC position statement) are designed to provide behavioral targets that may help children adopt healthy, active lifestyles. The guidelines are different than those for adults for the simple reason that children are different than adults. The amount of activity recommended for children (60 minutes) is greater than for adults since they have more time in the day and there is an important need to establish active patterns and promote motor skill development early in life. Consideration is also given to reducing levels of inactivity since excess inactivity (e.g., television and computer games) contributes to obesity and reduces children's opportunities for physical activity. The listing below summarizes the current COPEC/NASPE guidelines for physical activity. It is strongly recommended that you read the entire document and seek to apply the guidelines in your teaching.

If the central goal of physical education is the promotion of lifetime physical activity, then it is important to abide by and work to achieve established public health guidelines for physical activity. The accepted guideline for adults is to accumulate 30 minutes of physical activity on most, if not all, days of the week. The guideline was established jointly by the American College of Sports Medicine and the Centers for Disease Control and has been endorsed by a number of other professional and scientific organizations. The guidelines acknowledge that moderate-intensity physical activity can provide significant health benefits even if performed intermittently throughout the day. Emphasis is placed on getting all individuals to be somewhat active rather than to promote high levels of activity in subsamples of the population.

Summary of Guidelines for Appropriate Physical Activity for Elementary School Children

- Children should accumulate at least 60 minutes, and up to several hours, of age-appropriate physical activity on all or most days of the week. This daily accumulation should include moderate and vigorous physical activity of which the majority is intermittent in nature.

- Children should participate in several bouts of physical activity lasting 15 minutes or more each day.

- Children should participate each day in a variety of age-appropriate physical activities designed to achieve optimal health, wellness, fitness, and performance benefits.

- Extended periods (periods of two hours or more) of inactivity are discouraged for children, especially during the daytime hours.

It is well established that children are the most active segment of the population. According to estimates from large national surveys such as the Youth Risk Behavior Survey (YRBS), over 60% of youth (ages 14-18) indicate that they participate in vigorous physical activity three or more times per week. In contrast, recent estimates from the Department of Health and Human Services indicate that only 20% of American adults are sufficiently active. Most Americans do some activity, but a full 25% are reported to do little or no physical activity. Reports indicate that children's activity levels decline sharply during adolescence as they begin to take on adult responsibilities and adult lifestyle patterns. Clearly, a challenge for physical education teachers is to try to maintain a child's natural interest in activity over time.

The Youth Physical Activity Promotion Model

Public health officials have begun to emphasize the use of broad social-ecological approaches to promote health in the population. These models propose multiple dimensions of influence that are described as individual, interpersonal, organizational, community, and policy. Historically, the role of physical education has been aimed at the individual or interpersonal level as instruction and feedback are typically provided to individual students in small-group settings. In the broader social-ecological approach, teachers can have a greater influence if they adopt an expanded role as facilitators of family- and community-based physical activity and as champions of public policies that support quality physical education and quality physical activity programs for children. The Youth Physical Activity Promotion Model (Welk, 1999) provides a useful way to summarize the various factors that may influence children's interest and involvement in physical activity. The model distinguishes among factors thought to predispose, enable, and reinforce activity behavior in children and may be helpful in promoting physical activity in children (figure 3.1).

Predisposing Factors

Predisposing factors are elements that predispose a child to want to be physically active. This model reduces physical activity behavior to two fundamental questions: "Is it worth it?" and "Am I able?" The first question—"Is it worth it?"—addresses the benefits versus costs of participating in physical activity. This question reflects children's attitudes toward physical activity and the level of enjoyment they get from movement experiences. The question "Am I able?" addresses perceptions of competence. It is possible for a child to value physical activity but not feel capable of performing the activity competently. Because it is human nature to want to display competence and hide incompetence, children that feel unskilled in physical activities may not want to be active. In essence, it is important for children to be able to answer "yes" to both questions in order to be predisposed to physical activity.

Enabling Factors

Enabling factors are elements that enable a child to be physically active. This dimension includes environmental variables such as access to facilities, equipment, and programs that provide opportunities for physical activity. These variables directly influence a child's level of physical activity but do not ensure participation. Children who have access may not choose to make use of their resources, but if children do not have access they do not even have the opportunity. Physical skills and level of physical fitness are also considered enabling factors. Children who are physically fit and skilled are more likely to seek out opportunities to be active while children with poor fitness and skills are less likely to seek out these opportunities. This effect is most likely transmitted through the child's perception of competence ("Am I able?"). A child's perception of competence can have important consequences on that child's attraction to physical activity. Research has even confirmed that perceptions of competence may be more important than actual competence. Teachers can directly promote skills through effective instruction and constructive feedback.

Reinforcing Factors

Reinforcing factors are the variables that reinforce a child's interest and involvement in physical activity. Parents, peers, teachers, and coaches can all play a role in reinforcing a child's activity behavior. Reinforcing factors can influence a child's physical activity behavior directly and indirectly. The direct effect may stem from active encouragement by a parent or teacher to be physically active. The indirect effect stems from forces that shape a child's predisposition to physical activity. Reinforcement can shape a child's interest in physical activity ("Is it worth it?") as well as his or her perceptions of competence ("Am I able?"). At young ages, children may be more responsive to influence from teachers

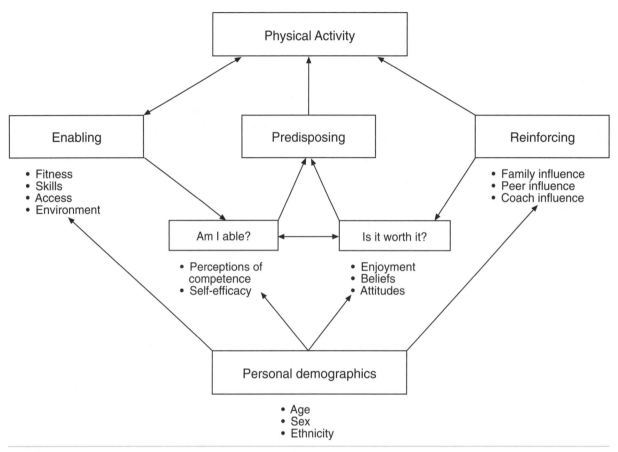

FIGURE 3.1   The Youth Physical Activity Promotion Model.

Adapted, by permission, from G. Welk, 1999, "The youth physical activity promotion model: A conceptual bridge between theory and practice," *Quest* 51: 5-23.

and parents. At older ages, peers probably exert a greater influence.

Applying the Youth Physical Activity Promotion Model

The paths proposed in figure 3.1 suggest that physical activity can be promoted in a variety of ways. The central influence on activity behavior is from the predisposing factors, since this domain reflects the child's personal attitudes toward and perceptions of physical activity. To most effectively promote interest and involvement in physical activity, the emphasis in physical education should be on experiences that promote a child's enjoyment of physical activity *("It is worth it!")* and perception of competence *("I am able!")*. The COPEC guidelines (Council for Physical Education for Children, 1998) provide valuable suggestions to ensure that physical activities are developmentally appropriate for children. Instructors are encouraged to seek out

these and other resources to help create programs that are educationally and motivationally sound for children.

Individual or Intrapersonal Promotion of Activity

As described in chapter 1, *FITNESSGRAM/ACTIVI-TYGRAM* has been rooted in the philosophy that health (H) is for everyone (E), is for a lifetime (L), and is personal (P). The primary objective of a fitness development program should be to establish regular activity habits through enjoyable physical activity experiences. The overall, long-term fitness objective for all students should be to develop or maintain a level of fitness within the Healthy Fitness Zone. Since being healthy is not a meaningful objective for most children, emphasis with children should be on objectives that are more relevant to their daily lives (e.g., looking good and feeling good). At an appropriate age, it is important for all children to understand that physical activity is necessary for good health. A key concept to communicate at this point is that maintaining a healthy fitness level does not require a tremendous amount of activity or time. Even those students who are not athletes and are not attracted to physical activity can easily do an adequate amount of activity to be healthy.

A unique aspect of the *FITNESSGRAM* software is that it allows students (through the student version of the program) to enter their own fitness results. The interactive software helps students learn more about the different dimensions of fitness and the importance of regular physical activity. By entering their own scores, students will also learn that fitness is personal. Because of the educational value for students, we advocate that students enter their own data. Some additional recommendations for promoting physical activity and physical fitness within physical education are as follows:

■ Provide a rationale for children to participate in regular physical activity. Make certain that the reasons are relevant to their daily life. The benefits of looking good, feeling good, and enjoying life are usually most salient with children.

■ Provide feedback regarding current status. Test results should be used for education about physical activity and fitness and for selecting areas in which to improve or maintain good performance.

■ Encourage students to establish short-term and long-term goals. Short-term goals are probably the most important and should be goals related to physical activity rather than goals related to fitness achievement. Instead of a goal to do five more sit-ups on the next test, a more appropriate **"process" goal** would be to perform abdominal strengthening activities three to four times each week. If a student works hard toward improving his or her fitness but does not manage to achieve the **"product" goal,** the result is a feeling of failure. A process goal allows the student to achieve success while slowly making progress toward the desired result. Goal-setting forms are included in appendix B on page 93.

■ Help each student identify a regular time and place to fit physical activity into their daily schedule. Talk about fitting activities into daily routines such as walking or biking to school, to a friend's house, or to the store. Part of making time for activity may be spending less time watching TV or playing video games.

■ Have students make a written commitment to participate in the activity required to achieve the goal. The activity should be enjoyable to the student. The list of activities should be a specific listing of the type of activity, day of the week, time of day, place, and other specific details.

■ Encourage students to keep track of their participation on a personal exercise log or through the *ACTIVITYGRAM* software.

■ Periodically ask students about their progress, showing that you are seriously interested in the program.

■ Discuss progress and problems. Being active is not easy for some. If a student is having difficulty meeting a goal, ask other students to suggest solutions.

■ Praise students for even small accomplishments in their efforts to achieve their goals. Feedback on success is very important in making children feel competent and thus establishing intrinsic motivation.

■ Recommend activities that are of low to moderate intensity since these activities are more likely to be maintained than some team sport activities. Activities such as walking and recreational bike riding are examples.

■ Be a role model to your class by including regular activity as a part of your lifestyle. Tell your students about your enjoyment of physical activity and its benefits.

Interpersonal and Institutional Promotion of Physical Activity

Because of time constraints, the promotion of physical activity must extend beyond the school and the school day and into the home and community. Collaborative efforts between schools and community programs are highlighted in the CDC's guidelines for school and community physical activity programs (Centers for Disease Control and Prevention, 1997). Specifically, these guidelines recommend that physical activity be promoted through a coordinated school health program and with links established between the school, family, and community. Physical education teachers can and should play a central role in the development of these links. In this view, the role of physical education broadens to include outreach goals that integrate school, family, and community programs. Descriptions of successful programs that fulfill aspects of these guidelines are described in a book called *Active Youth* (Human Kinetics, 1998). The following listing provides some specific suggestions for how teachers can promote activity outside of school.

■ Teach parents about the important role they play in shaping a child's interest in and enjoyment of physical activity. Ideally, families should try to do activities together. Evening and weekend outings are enjoyable. If the whole family cannot participate together, encourage activity in pairs.

■ Encourage family support of children's efforts to be active. Praise and encouragement are more effective than nagging. Parents can transport children to activity sessions and take them to parks to play. Children can also be asked to help parents with chores so parents have time for activity.

■ Involve parents as much as possible in promotional efforts through physical education. Sending home *FITNESSGRAM* reports and providing e-mail updates or reminders to parents may be useful ways of promoting greater parental involvement.

■ Become linked to the recreation programs and sport programs available in the community. Provide in-service training to volunteer coaches so that they may become more aware of how to promote lifelong activity in children and not just success in sport.

Reinforcement (Recognition and Motivation)

An integral part of fitness and activity programs is providing motivation to children and youth, which will encourage them to participate in the activity necessary to produce the desired fitness outcomes. One method of motivating participants is to recognize them for their successes.

In the past, the basis of most recognition programs has usually been fitness performance (the product). A more appropriate method is to use recognition programs based on participating regularly in physical activity (the process) as this is more likely to track into adulthood. Children and youth who are consistently active (the process) will achieve good fitness (the product) to the extent that heredity, maturation, and other factors allow. The *FITNESSGRAM* program strongly encourages process-based recognition in physical education. Performance recognition is also acceptable but generally should not be used to the exclusion of recognition for being regularly active. The following paragraphs present the rationale for using a system of recognition based on behavior rather than performance.

■ To be effective, recognition must be based on achievement of goals that are challenging yet attainable. Goals that are too hard are not motivating and can result in lack of effort. This is especially true for students with low physical self-esteem—often the children and youth who are in most need of improved fitness. Challenging yet achievable goals are intrinsically motivating.

■ If a recognition system is not based on goals that seem attainable, children and youth will not be motivated to give effort. When effort ceases to pay off, children may develop "learned helplessness." Learned helplessness occurs when children perceive that there is no reason to try because trying does not result in reaching the goal. The best way to treat learned helplessness is to reward "mastery attempts" (effort or process) rather than "mastery" (performance or product).

■ Intrinsic motivation for any behavior, including exercise and physical fitness behaviors, must be based on continuous feedback of progress (information). Awards that are perceived as controlling rather than informative do not build intrinsic motivation. Awards based on test performance provide little feedback concerning the person's progress toward the goal. Recognition of behavior can provide day-to-day feedback in terms of progress and information about personal achievement and competence that can be intrinsically motivating. Intrinsic motivation is evidenced by feelings of competence, willingness to give effort, a perception that exercise is important, lack of anxiety in activity, and enjoyment of activity.

■ Awards that are given to those with exceptionally high scores on fitness tests often go to those who have the gift of exceptional heredity and early maturity and to those already receiving many rewards for their physical accomplishments. Research indicates that awards or recognition given for exceptional performance are available to very small numbers of people. The result is a loss of motivation among many.

The Presidential Active Lifestyle Award (PALA) from the President's Council on Physical Fitness and Sports (PCPFS) provides a process-based award as part of its recognition program. The *FITNESSGRAM* has not historically focused on or endorsed recognition systems by the PCPFS for fitness, but this activity-based program is consistent with the *FITNESSGRAM* philosophy. The *FITNESSGRAM/ACTIVITYGRAM* program and the related Physical Best curriculum from the American Alliance for Health, Physical Education, Recreation and Dance have established a working relationship with the

TABLE 3.1	Goal Setting Criteria to Qualify for PALA	
	Males	**Females**
First six weeks	11,000 steps	9,000 steps
Second six weeks	12,000 steps	10,000 steps
Third six weeks	13,000 steps	11,000 steps

PCPFS to use PALA as the motivational complement for our programs. Used properly, PALA can assist in providing the basis for sound education about essential fitness concepts and can motivate students to become and stay active for a lifetime. The sections that follow summarize this award program and provide suggestions for funding the program in your school.

Description of the Presidential Active Lifestyle Award

The Presidential Active Lifestyle Award (PALA) recognizes youth ages 6 through 17 for establishing and maintaining a physically active lifestyle. Students are asked to track either steps per day from a pedometer or minutes of activity per day. For students just getting started, PALA can be earned by establishing and achieving specific activity goals (see table 3.1). The activity goals in PALA are to achieve 60 minutes of activity a day or a specific daily step total based on a pedometer (11,000 steps for girls and 13,000 steps for boys). Students who reach the activity goals five days each week for a six-week period can earn the PALA award. Award items include the PALA patch, a certificate, or both. Other recognition items are also available.

The Active Lifestyle Model School program is also a part of PALA. In addition there is a program to recognize adults for regular physical activity—a wonderful tool to encourage parents to be active with their children. Additional information about PALA is available at www.presidentschallenge.org.

Funding the PALA Recognition Program

If your budget will not allow the school to purchase Presidential Active Lifestyle Awards, alternative sources of funding may be available. Parent-teacher associations/organizations are often willing to support incentives for children in the school. Local businesses and community service clubs (e.g., Kiwanis, Rotary, Lions) are also interested in assisting with school-related projects, especially when they can affect students throughout the community. When approaching other organizations, be certain to explain the following concepts of *ACTIVITYGRAM*, Physical Best, and PALA:

- Emphasis on development of exercise behavior rather than performance
- High probability for motivating all students with reasonable standards and goals
- High probability that most students can be successful regardless of their skill level or their personal interests

Presidential Youth Fitness Program

Most students who participate in physical activity almost every day will be able to achieve a score that will place them in the Healthy Fitness Zone® (HFZ). A student who scores in the HFZ in 5 out of 6 events is eligible to receive the Presidential Youth Fitness Award. Go to http://www.presidentialyouth fitnessprogram.org/recognition to learn more.

Summary

Research evidence suggests that children are highly active but become less active with age as they adopt adult patterns of living. Efforts are needed to maintain children's natural interest in physical activity over time so that they become active and healthy adults. The direct emphasis on principles of physical activity promotion outlined in this chapter can be useful in this regard.

PART II

FITNESSGRAM ASSESSMENT MODULE

The *FITNESSGRAM* assessment measures three components of physical fitness that have been identified as important because of their relationship to overall health and optimal function. The three components are aerobic capacity; body composition; and muscular strength, endurance, and flexibility. Several test options are provided for most areas, with one test item being recommended. Each item is scored using criterion-referenced standards that are established based on the level of fitness needed for good health. Research and validation work conducted over many years has helped to refine these standards so that there are separate criteria for boys and girls at different ages. Because only modest amounts of activity are needed to obtain health benefits, most students who perform regular physical activity will be able to achieve a score that will place them within or above the Healthy Fitness Zone (HFZ) on all *FITNESSGRAM* test items.

Chapter 4 covers general principles associated with conducting fitness testing. It provides guidelines for testing primary students as well as general guidelines for safety. Chapters 5, 6, and 7 give detailed information on assessments of aerobic capacity, body composition, and musculoskeletal fitness, respectively. Chapter 8 provides information on the physical activity questionnaire in *FITNESSGRAM*. Chapter 9 focuses on interpreting *FITNESSGRAM* test results.

CHAPTER 4

FITNESSGRAM TEST ADMINISTRATION

This chapter describes basic considerations for administering and scoring fitness test items. Appendix B contains samples of class score sheets and individual score sheets for self-assessment. The *FITNESSGRAM* software will also print a class score sheet. Table 4.1 provides a summary list of the test items. In addition to the test scores, the *FITNESSGRAM* software requires the following student information: first name, last name, gender, birth date, and grade.

An important component of the *FITNESSGRAM* software is the inclusion of physical activity assessments. While fitness is important, it cannot be maintained unless children are physically active. Benefits associated with physical activity are also independent of those that come from participation in regular physical activity. The *FITNESSGRAM* software includes specific algorithms that take into account a child's activity and fitness level when providing individualized feedback. Additional information on the questions is available in chapter 8, and information on the feedback algorithms is in chapter 9.

This chapter provides information on how to administer the *FITNESSGRAM* battery in an efficient and organized manner.

Considerations for Testing Primary Grades

The major emphasis when testing children in grades K-3 should be on enjoyment and instructions on proper technique. It is important at this age not to focus on performance level. Performance standards are not available for the aerobic capacity test items for students younger than 10 years of age. While standards are provided for other test items for primary grade children, you are strongly encouraged not to emphasize performance level and test results.

Considerations for Safety

The test items used in *FITNESSGRAM* have been administered to millions of students and have

TABLE 4.1   ***FITNESSGRAM* Test Items**

| Aerobic capacity | Body composition | Muscular strength, endurance, and flexibility | | | |
		Abdominal strength and endurance	Trunk extensor strength and flexibility	Upper body strength and endurance	Flexibility
The PACER*	Skinfold measure-ments*	Curl-up*	Trunk lift*	90° push-up*	Back-saver sit and reach
One-mile run	Body mass index			Modified pull-up	Shoulder stretch
The walk test (secondary students)	Bioelectric impedance analyzers			Flexed arm hang	

*Recommended test.

been shown to be very safe. The prudent teacher, however, will recognize that with any strenuous physical activity there is always the possibility that incidents may occur.

Before administering any test items, be aware of the potential health problems of all students in your classes. For example, it is possible for a student to have a congenital heart condition that may require special consideration during the administration of an aerobic capacity measure or other test items. Maximizing the safety of all students should be the primary objective.

Your school district or agency should have established policies related to medical information, medical records, and medical clearance for activity. It is important that you be aware of these policies and that you follow them strictly.

It is also important that students be conditioned adequately before taking the test. This conditioning period is especially important during the fall of the year and in hotter climates.

Considerations for Testing Special Populations

FITNESSGRAM is intended for use with students who do not have disabilities. You will, in many situations, also be working with students with disabilities. If certain physical fitness components are deemed important as a dimension in education, they are equally important for all students. We suggest, therefore, that teachers needing assistance in developing tasks for an assessment should consult one of these excellent resources: *Brockport Physical Fitness Test Kit, The Brockport Physical Fitness Test Manual*, and *The Brockport Physical Fitness Training Guide* (Winnick and Short, 1999). The software program with these materials has been designed so that you can easily share student data with the *FITNESSGRAM/ACTIVITYGRAM* software.

Need Additional Information?

To order the Brockport resources, call Human Kinetics at 800-747-4457 ext 5555, or order online at www.HumanKinetics.com.

CHAPTER 5

AEROBIC CAPACITY

Aerobic capacity is perhaps the most important component of any fitness program. Research indicates that acceptable levels of aerobic capacity are associated with a reduced risk of high blood pressure, coronary heart disease, obesity, diabetes, some forms of cancer, and other health problems in adults. The evidence documenting the health benefits of physical activity has been well described, and this information was the basis for the development of the U.S. physical activity guidelines and other similar public health recommendations for physical activity.

Many terms have been used to describe this dimension of physical fitness, including cardiovascular fitness, cardiorespiratory fitness, cardiorespiratory endurance, aerobic fitness, aerobic work capacity, and physical working capacity. Although defined somewhat differently, these terms can generally be considered synonymous with aerobic capacity. A laboratory measure of maximal oxygen uptake ($\dot{V}O_2max$) is generally considered to be the best measure of aerobic capacity. Because differences in body size can influence oxygen uptake, aerobic capacity is typically expressed relative to body weight (i.e., milliliters O_2 consumed per kilogram of body weight per minute, or $ml \cdot kg^{-1} \cdot min^{-1}$).

The *FITNESSGRAM* program provides three field tests of aerobic capacity (PACER, one-mile run/walk, and walk test). Beginning with version 8.6 and version 9 of the *FITNESSGRAM* software, estimates of aerobic capacity are reported as $\dot{V}O_2max$ and expressed as $ml \cdot kg^{-1} \cdot min^{-1}$. For the one-mile run/walk and the walk test, calculation of aerobic capacity requires the use of BMI (which is calculated from height and weight). Therefore, entry of height and weight are required in order to estimate $\dot{V}O_2max$ when these tests are used. High test–retest reliability and accurate estimates of measured $\dot{V}O_2max$ have been demonstrated for all measures of aerobic capacity. The following sections provide guidelines for administering and scoring all three tests.

Need Additional Information?

For additional information on the three tests, see the *FITNESSGRAM Reference Guide*. The *guide* is available on the enclosed DVD or online at the *FITNESSGRAM* website, www.fitnessgram.net (go to the *Reference Guide* section). Read the chapter titled "Aerobic Capacity Assessments" by Cureton and Plowman.

Overview of the FITNESSGRAM Aerobic Capacity Standards

The *FITNESSGRAM* Scientific Advisory Board has worked to ensure that all of the assessments in fitness are scored using health-related standards. The availability of nationally representative data on fitness from the National Health and Nutrition Examination Survey (NHANES) made it possible to develop objective health standards for aerobic fitness when expressed as $\dot{V}O_2$max. Detailed information on the development of the standards is provided in the Reference Guide and in a comprehensive research supplement published in the *American Journal of Preventive Medicine*. Several key points associated with the aerobic fitness standards are summarized here:

1. Estimates of aerobic capacity are expressed as $\dot{V}O_2$max in ml·kg–1·min–1, regardless of what assessment was used. The $\dot{V}O_2$max is estimated from equations developed specifically for the PACER or one-mile run/walk. For the one-mile run/walk, time, age, sex, height, and weight need to be entered into the program in order to receive an estimate of $\dot{V}O_2$max. For the PACER, laps completed, age, and sex are required in order to receive an estimate of $\dot{V}O_2$max.

2. The health-related standards used to evaluate aerobic capacity are age and sex specific and also take into account normal changes during growth and maturation. The values for boys increase with age, while the values for girls decrease with age. These changes do not imply higher expectations for boys and lower expectations for girls. The changes are reflective of the natural developmental trends for boys and girls (boys gain muscle with age while girls tend to gain body fat through adolescence). The lines actually reflect the same relative level of fitness across age for both boys and girls.

3. The new standards are equivalent for 10- and 11-year-old boys and girls. From a developmental perspective, boys and girls are more similar than different at these young ages. As they mature, boys and girls follow different developmental trends, so the fitness standards would follow these tracks.

4. The new standards allow classification into three unique zones (rather than two) with the use of two parallel lines. Students who have scores above the top line for their sex would be classified in the **Healthy Fitness Zone**. A child above this line would be classified as having sufficient fitness for good health. Students who have scores between the two lines would be classified in the **Needs Improvement** and receive a message that they should work to reach the Healthy Fitness Zone. Students below the bottom line would be classified in the **Needs Improvement—Health Risk** zone. This lowest fitness zone would provide youth and parents with an appropriate warning that this low level of fitness increases health risks. The use of three distinct fitness zones makes it possible to provide more specific information about health and potential health risks. Students in the HFZ are provided with feedback to maintain their fitness, while students in the Needs Improvement zone are appropriately warned about possible health risks if their fitness remains low.

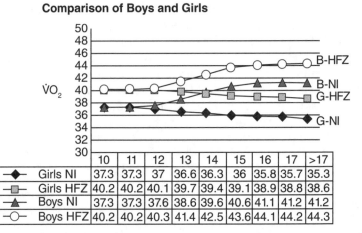

Comparison of Boys and Girls

		10	11	12	13	14	15	16	17	>17
◆	Girls NI	37.3	37.3	37	36.6	36.3	36	35.8	35.7	35.3
■	Girls HFZ	40.2	40.2	40.1	39.7	39.4	39.1	38.9	38.8	38.6
▲	Boys NI	37.3	37.3	37.6	38.6	39.6	40.6	41.1	41.2	41.2
○	Boys HFZ	40.2	40.2	40.3	41.4	42.5	43.6	44.1	44.2	44.3

PACER

⇨ *Recommended*

The PACER (Progressive Aerobic Cardiovascular Endurance Run) is the default aerobic capacity test in *FITNESSGRAM*. The PACER is a multistage fitness test adapted from the 20-meter shuttle run test published by Leger and Lambert (1982) and revised in 1988 (Leger et al.). The test is progressive in intensity—it is easy at the beginning and gets more difficult at the end. The progressive nature of the test provides a built-in warm-up and helps children to pace themselves. The test has also been set to music to create a valid, fun alternative to the customary distance run test for measuring aerobic capacity. Information on obtaining the music CD can be found in appendix A on page 85.

The PACER is recommended for all ages, but its use is strongly recommended for participants in grades K-3. The PACER is recommended for a number of reasons, including the following:

- All students are more likely to have a positive experience in performing the PACER.
- The PACER helps students learn the skill of pacing.
- Students who have a poorer performance will finish first and not be subjected to the embarrassment of being the last person to complete the test.

When you are administering the test to these younger children, the emphasis should be on allowing the children to have a good time while learning how to take this test and pace themselves. Allow children to continue to run as long as they wish and as long as they are still enjoying the activity. The main goal for young children is to allow them the opportunity to experience the assessment and to enjoy it.

Test Objective

The objective is to run as long as possible with continuous movement back and forth across a 20-meter space at a specified pace that gets faster each minute. A 15-meter version of the PACER test has been developed for teachers with smaller-sized facilities. To enter 15-meter scores into the 8.x software, a conversion chart is available on page 98. The music CD is now available.

Equipment and Facilities

Administering the PACER requires a flat, nonslip surface at least 20 meters long, CD or cassette player with adequate volume, CD or audiocassette, measuring tape, marker cones, pencil, and copies of score sheet A or B (found in appendix B). Students should wear shoes with nonslip soles. Plan for each student to have a 40- to 60-inch-wide space for running. An outdoor area can be used for this test if you do not have adequate indoor space. There should be a designated area for runners who have finished and for scorekeepers. You may want to paint lines or draw chalk lines to assist students in running in a straight line.

Note: Because many gyms are not 20 meters in length, an alternative 15-meter PACER test CD is now available. The procedures described as follows are the same for the 15-meter distance, but an alternative CD and scoring sheet are required for tracking the number of laps. To enter 15-meter scores into the 8.0 software, a conversion chart is available on page 98. The music CD is now available. The 15-meter PACER test is for use only in elementary schools.

Test Instructions

- Mark the 20-meter (21-yard, 32-inch) course with marker cones to divide lanes and use a tape or chalk line at each end.
- Make copies of score sheet A or B for each group of students to be tested.
- Before test day, allow students to listen to several minutes of the tape so that they know what to expect. Students should then be allowed at least two practice sessions.
- Allow students to select a partner. Have students who are being tested line up behind the start line.
- The individual PACER CDs have two music versions: one with only the beeps and one with the cadences for the push-up and curl-up tests. Each version of the test will give a 5-second countdown and tell the students when to start.
- Each student being tested should run across the 20-meter distance and touch the line with a foot by the time the beep sounds. The student should take full weight on the foot that is touching the line. At the sound of the beep, the student turns around and runs back to the other end. If some students get to the line before the beep, they must wait for the beep before running the other direction. Students continue in this manner until they fail to reach the line before the beep for the second time. A diagram of the PACER test is on page 31.

(continued)

PACER *(continued)*

- A single beep will sound at the end of the time for each lap. A triple beep sounds at the end of each minute. The triple beep serves the same function as the single beep and also alerts the runners that the pace will get faster. Inform students that when the triple beep sounds, they should not stop but should continue the test by turning and running toward the other end of the area.

- Scoring the PACER will require the input of each student's height and weight. Calculation of aerobic capacity requires a score of at least 10 laps (20-meter version).

When to Stop

The first time a student does not reach the line by the time of the beep, the student stops where he or she is and reverses direction immediately, attempting to get back on pace. The test is completed for a student the next time (second time) he or she fails to reach the line by the time of the beep (the two misses do not have to be consecutive; the test is over after two total misses). Students just completing the test should continue to walk and stretch in the designated cool-down area. Figure 5.1 provides diagrams of testing procedures.

Note: A student who remains at one end of the testing area through two beeps (does not run to the other end and back) should be scored as having two misses and the test is over.

Scoring

In the PACER test, a lap is one 20-meter distance (from one end to the other). The scorer records the lap number (crossing off each lap number) on a PACER score sheet (samples provided in appendix B). The recorded score is the total number of laps completed by the student. For ease in administration, it is permissible to count the first miss (not making the line by the time of the beep). It is important to be consistent with all of the students and classes in the method used for counting.

An alternative scoring method is available. This method does not eliminate students when they miss their second beep (Schiemer, 1996). Using the PACER score sheet B, establish two different symbols to be used in recording, such as a star for making the line by the time of the beep and a tri-

angle for not making the line. The scorer then draws a star in the circle when the runner makes the line by the time of the beep and a triangle when the runner fails to make the line by the time of the beep, simply making a record of what occurs. The runners can continue to participate until the leader stops the music or until they voluntarily stop running. To determine the score, find the second triangle (or whatever symbol was used). The number associated with the preceding star is the score. An example is provided in figure 5.2.

Regardless of the method, the scoring of the PACER test is based on the number of laps completed. Therefore, the laps have to be directly entered into the software. It is important to count each individual 15-meter or 20-meter distance as a lap (rather than based on a down-and-back count for the laps). The software will use the number of laps completed along with the child's age to estimate aerobic capacity, and this will be used to generate individualized feedback on the reports.

Criterion standards are not available for students in grades K-3. The object of the test for these younger students is simply to have them participate in the testing process and to complete as many laps as possible. The main goal is to provide the students with the opportunity to experience the PACER and to have a positive experience with the assessment. Nine-year-olds in grade 4 will receive a score, and it will be evaluated against a criterion standard. All 10-year-old students receive a score regardless of grade level.

Suggestions for Test Administration

- Both PACER CDs contain 21 levels (1 level per minute for 21 minutes). During the first minute, the 20-meter version allows 9 seconds to run the distance; the 15-meter version allows 6.75 seconds. The lap time decreases by approximately half a second at each successive level. Make certain that students have practiced and understand that the speed will increase each minute.

- A single beep indicates the end of a lap (one 20-meter distance). The students run from one end to the other between each beep. Caution students not to begin too fast. The beginning speed is very slow. Nine seconds is allowed for running each 20-meter lap during the first minute.

(continued)

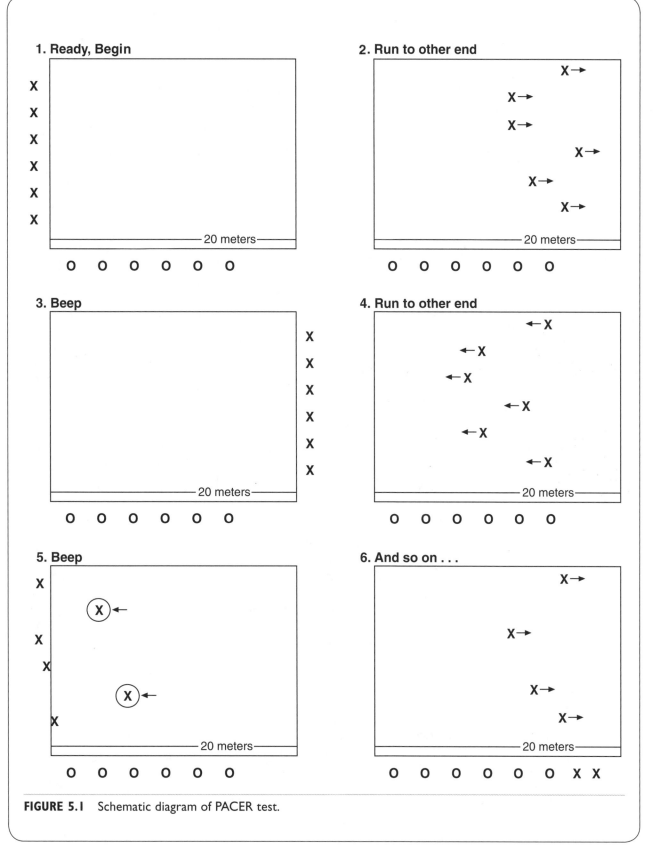

FIGURE 5.1 Schematic diagram of PACER test.

(*continued*)

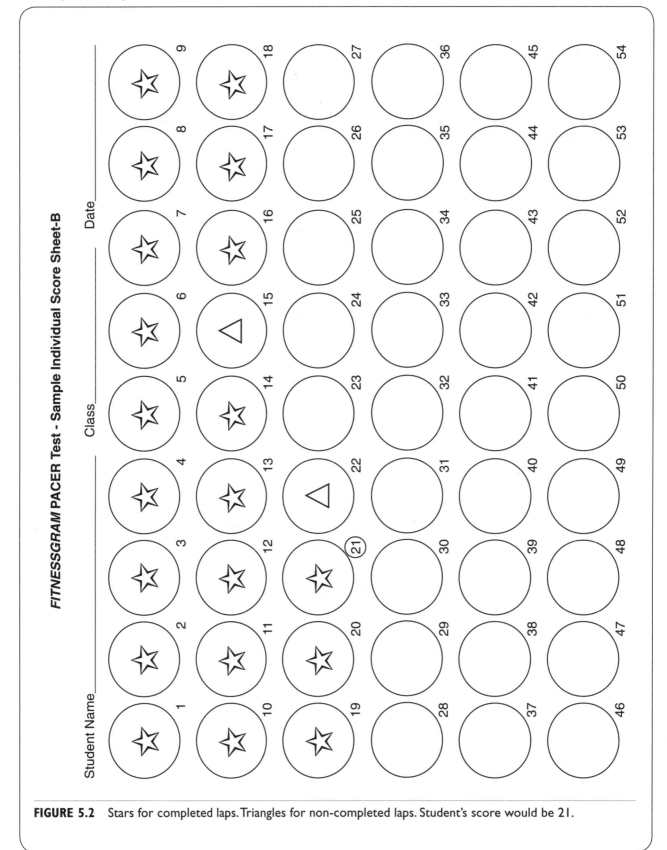

FITNESSGRAM PACER Test - Sample Individual Score Sheet-B

Student Name

Class

Date

FIGURE 5.2 Stars for completed laps. Triangles for non-completed laps. Student's score would be 21.

(continued)

PACER *(continued)*

- Triple beeps at the end of each minute indicate the end of a level and an increase in speed. Students should be alerted that the speed will increase. When students hear the triple beeps they should turn around at the line and immediately continue running. Some students have a tendency to hesitate when they hear the triple beeps.

- A student who cannot reach the line when the beep sounds should be given one more chance to regain the pace. The second time a student cannot reach the line by the time of the beep, his or her test is completed.

- Groups of students may be tested at one time. Adult volunteers may be asked to help record scores. Students may record scores for each other or for younger students.

- Each runner must be allowed a path 40 to 60 inches wide. It may work best to mark the course.

- If using the audiotape, you may save time by using two tapes and two cassette players. Rewind the first tape while the second group is running the tests, and so forth. Using the CD is a much more efficient method for administering this test item.

One-Mile Run

⇨ *Alternative*

The one-mile run can be used instead of the PACER to provide an estimate of aerobic capacity ($\dot{V}O_2$max). For students who enjoy running and are highly motivated, it is a very good alternative assessment. Scoring of the one-mile run will require the input of a student's height and weight since the calculation of aerobic capacity includes BMI.

Test Objective

The objective of the assessment is to run a mile at the fastest pace possible (i.e., shortest time). If a student gets tired, it is okay to allow him or her to walk, but encourage the student to try to at least maintain a slow jog throughout the assessment. An aerobic capacity score cannot be obtained for mile times greater than 13:00, and this time would not likely be achieved at a walking pace. If students cannot complete a one-mile jog or run, they should be encouraged to complete the one-mile walk test. Note that the walk test is validated only for those age 13 and older.

Equipment and Facilities

A flat and accurately measured running course, stopwatch, pencil, and score sheets (included in appendix B) are required. The course may be a track or any other measured area. The course may be measured using a tape measure or cross country wheel. Caution: If the track is metric or shorter than 440 yards, adjust the running course (1,609.34 meters = 1 mile; 400 meters = 437.4 yards; 1,760 yards =

1 mile). On a 400-meter track the run should be four laps plus 10 yards.

Test Instructions

Describe the course to the students, and encourage them to complete the distance in the shortest possible time. Remind them to listen for their time as they cross the line. Also, many students begin too fast and tire out, so it is important to remind them to use appropriate pacing to get an accurate assessment. To initiate the assessments, you can provide a signal of "Ready . . . start." As they cross the finish line, elapsed time should be called out to the participants (or their partners) and then recorded.

Scoring

The scoring of the one-mile run is based on the total time as well as the child's age, sex, and BMI (obtained from height and weight); these data need to be entered into the software. The software will use the entered data to estimate the child's aerobic capacity. The score will then be used in the software to determine what fitness zone the child is placed into and what feedback is provided.

Criterion standards are not available for students in grades K-3 (ages 5-9). The object of the test for these younger students is simply to complete the one-mile distance at a comfortable pace and to practice pacing (photo 5.1), so it is not necessary to time the run for these students. The time *can* be entered into the software, but a performance standard will not be used to evaluate their score. Nine-year-olds in grade 4 will receive a standard. All 10-year-olds should receive a score regardless of grade level.

(continued)

One-Mile Run (*continued*)

Remember that the height and weight for each student must be entered in addition to the performance time on the one-mile run. Calculation of aerobic capacity also requires a time less than 13:01. A child scoring above this time will be placed into the Needs Improvement—Health Risk zone since this achievement would result in an estimate of aerobic capacity below the health standard.

Suggestions for Test Administration

- Call out times as the runners pass the start-and-stop line to assist students in pacing themselves.

- Preparation for the test should include instruction about pacing and practice in pacing. Without instruction, students usually run too fast early in the test and then are forced to walk near the end.

- Results are generally better if a student can maintain a constant pace during most of the test.

- Walking is certainly permitted, but students should be encouraged to complete the assessment at a slow jog rather than a walking pace. If students can't complete a mile, they should be assessed with the one-mile walk test, although that test is validated only for ages 13 and older.

- Have students set a goal before running.

- Students should always warm up before taking the test. They should also cool down by continuing to walk for several minutes after completing the distance. A good suggestion is to have those who have completed the distance do an easy activity (juggle, hula hoop) while waiting for others to complete the distance. This keeps everyone moving and busy and takes the focus off the slower students who will complete the distance last.

- Avoid administering the test under conditions of unusually high temperature or humidity or when the wind is strong, because these elements may be unsafe or may lead to an invalid estimate of aerobic capacity.

- Counting laps completed and accurately recording the run time can be a problem when a relatively small course is used with younger children. Many techniques are acceptable. Pair the students and have the resting partner count laps and record time for the runner. Older students or parents may be asked to assist in recording results for younger students. Appendix B contains a sample scoring and recording sheet.

PHOTO 5.1   Student running.

Walk Test

⇨ *Alternative*

Another alternative to the PACER test is the one-mile walk test. This test is only for students ages 13 and older since it hasn't been validated with younger samples. The walk test is an excellent alternative assessment because it can be used for a lifetime. Secondary students should learn to do this test because it is one that they can repeat on their own to self-assess their fitness levels.

Test Objective

The objective is to walk one mile as quickly as possible while maintaining a constant walking pace for the entire distance. The assessment is based on the relative heart rate for a given speed of walking, so the actual pace is not critical. This test is included

(*continued*)

Walk Test *(continued)*

in *FITNESSGRAM* for use with participants ages 13 years and older. The walk test is an excellent self-assessment skill for everyone to use throughout life.

Equipment and Facilities

A flat, accurately measured (1 mile) course, two or more stopwatches, pencils, and score sheets (included in appendix B) are required. Heart rate monitors, if available, make heart rate monitoring much easier. The course may be measured using a tape measure or cross country wheel. Caution: If the track is metric or shorter than 440 yards, adjust the course (1,609.34 meters = 1 mile; 400 meters = 437.4 yards; 1,760 yards = 1 mile). On a 400-meter track the walk should be four laps plus 10 yards.

Test Instructions

Describe the course to the students, and instruct them to complete the full mile at a steady, brisk walking pace that can be maintained the entire distance (photo 5.2). As they cross the finish line, elapsed time should be called to the participants (or their partners). It is possible to test 15 to 30 students at one time by dividing the group. Have each student select a partner; one is the walker and one is the scorer. While one group walks, the scorers count laps and record the finish time. Appendix B contains a sample score sheet for scorers to use.

At the conclusion of the one-mile walk, each student should take a 60-second heart rate count. The scorer can time the 60 seconds, or students can count the time themselves by using a pace clock with a second hand. If using heart rate monitors to determine the heart rate, each participant should start his or her stopwatch at the beginning of the walk and stop it at the end. The last heart rate recorded during the walk should be used as the walking heart rate.

Scoring

The walk test is based on the relative heart rate in walking a mile at a specific speed. Therefore, it is important to have an accurate measure of the mile walk time (scored in minutes and seconds) as well as a 60-second heart rate. The walk time and 60-second heart rate are entered in the *FITNESS-GRAM* software, and the child's estimated $\dot{V}O_2$max is calculated using the Rockport Fitness Walking Test equation (Kline et al. 1987; McSwegin et al.

PHOTO 5.2   Student walking.

1998). The estimate is evaluated using the same aerobic fitness standards as the other assessments, and this is used to determine the feedback messages provided on the reports.

Suggestions for Test Administration

■ Preparation for the test should include instruction and practice in pacing and in techniques for heart rate monitoring.

■ Results are generally better if the student can maintain a constant pace during most of the test.

■ Students should always warm up before taking the test. They should also cool down by continuing to walk for several minutes after completing the distance.

■ Avoid administering the test under conditions of unusually high temperature or humidity or when the wind is strong, because these elements may cause an invalid estimate of aerobic capacity.

CHAPTER 6

BODY COMPOSITION

Body composition refers to the division of total body weight (mass) into components, most commonly fat mass and fat-free mass. The proportion of total body weight that is fat (referred to as percent body fat) is an important health-related indicator because high levels of body fatness are associated with increased risk of coronary heart disease, stroke, and diabetes. While children are not generally at risk for heart disease or stroke, elevated blood pressure and cholesterol occur in overweight and obese children. In addition, type 2 diabetes has increasingly been diagnosed among children, even though this condition has generally been viewed as "adult-onset" diabetes. Risk factors for obesity and heart disease are known to track through the life span, so it is important to document body composition as part of a comprehensive health-related fitness profile. Like other dimensions of health-related fitness, body composition does affect health status (even in childhood) and does improve with regular participation in physical activity.

A number of methods are available for estimating body fatness, but the most commonly used field measures are skinfold measurements and bioelectrical impedance analyzers. The skinfold approach involves the measurement of skinfold thicknesses at different parts of the body using a calibrated measurement tool called a caliper. The *FITNESSGRAM* skinfold procedure uses two sites that are easy to measure and whose measurements are not very invasive (triceps and calf). The measurements from these sites are then used in prediction equations to estimate body fatness. Bioelectric impedance analyzers use a very different approach to estimate body fatness. The devices send a small current through the body and measure resistance to current flow. A body with more muscle will have lower resistance to current flow, whereas a body with more fat will have greater resistance to current flow. While originally used only in research, a number of portable bioelectric impedance analyzer (BIA) devices are now commercially available at a price that is reasonable for most physical education programs (<$100). Because these devices can produce estimates of body composition faster than a skinfold test and do not require specific skill or experience, they may be a useful alternative to skinfold testing in some schools. The procedure is also less invasive than skinfold testing and may be better accepted in some districts that have specific policies against the use of skinfold calipers. However, the intuitive nature of skinfold testing also provides some unique educational advantages. Regardless of which approach is used, it is important to note that the estimates can vary by 2% to 3% of actual values.

Body mass index (BMI) is another indicator of body composition used in the *FITNESSGRAM* software. It is a commonly used index that provides an estimate of the appropriateness of a person's weight in relation to his or her height. While it technically does not reflect body composition, it is an assessment that is widely used in determining weight status (e.g., overweight or obesity). The use of BMI may lead to inaccurate classifications of body composition in heavily muscled individuals, but it provides a good indicator of body composition for the majority of the population. An advantage of using BMI is that it allows for more direct comparisons with public health data released from state and national health departments. The *FITNESSGRAM*

Scientific Advisory Board has historically recommended the reporting of body fat for assessments of body composition, but the popularity and ease of obtaining estimates of BMI make this an appropriate and acceptable measure. Details on collecting and scoring these assessments of body composition are provided in the following sections.

Need Additional Information?

For additional information on the advantages and disadvantages of various body composition measures and justification for the *FITNESSGRAM* Healthy Fitness Zone criteria, visit the *FITNESSGRAM* Reference Guide. The guide is available on the enclosed DVD or online at the *FITNESSGRAM* website, www.fitnessgram.net (go to the Reference Guide section). Read the chapter "Body Composition Assessments" by Going, Lohman, and Falls.

Overview of the FITNESSGRAM Body Composition Standards

The use of criterion-referenced standards is a defining characteristic of the *FITNESSGRAM* program. Members of the *FITNESSGRAM* Scientific Advisory Board used data from the National Health and Nutrition Examination Survey (NHANES) to develop the *FITNESSGRAM* standards for body fatness. A unique advantage of the NHANES data set is that the data are based on a representative sample of children and youth from across the United States. The *FITNESSGRAM* body fat standards take growth and maturation into account and reflect a child's current risk for metabolic syndrome—a significant health problem that is viewed as a precursor to the development of diabetes. Detailed information on the development of the body fat standards is provided in the Reference Guide and in a comprehensive research supplement published in the *American Journal of Preventive Medicine*.

A parallel set of *FITNESSGRAM* BMI standards correspond with the standards established for body fatness, but a limitation is that they differed from the widely used CDC growth charts, which are commonly used by pediatricians. Although the differences between the CDC values and the *FITNESSGRAM* standards were small in absolute terms, it caused some children to be classified differently using the two methods. Therefore, the Cooper Institute commissioned an additional set of analyses to directly compare the predictive utility of the *FITNESSGRAM* standards with the CDC values. The study used additional rounds of NHANES data and directly evaluated the classification differences of the alternative schemes. The analyses revealed that there were no statistically significant differences between the approaches and they both had similar clinical utility. Therefore, the CDC standards have been adopted as the BMI standards in *FITNESSGRAM*. The adoption of these commonly used BMI standards will enable youth to receive consistent information from *FITNESSGRAM* and the CDC growth charts.

The *FITNESSGRAM* body fat standards allow classification in three unique zones, and these can be operationalized similarly to the commonly used terms of normal weight, overweight, and obese. In this case, students are placed in the **Healthy Fitness Zone** if they have a healthy level of body fatness or a normal weight classification according to the CDC BMI values. Similarly, a child would be

(continued)

placed into the **Needs Improvement** zone if he is in the overweight category and in the **Needs Improvement—Health Risk** zone if he is in the obese category. With body composition, there are also risks associated with being too lean, so there is a zone called **Very Lean**. Youth who score in this category will receive feedback about the importance of healthy eating and activity. While there are children who are naturally very lean, it is important to make parents aware that their children's body composition places them in this category.

It is important to recognize that body fat and BMI provide different perspectives about a child's body composition. The two assessments are based on different measures and cannot be expected to provide consistent information for all youth or to provide similar group distributions. However, the standards have been set up so that the BMI standards can be interpreted in a similar way as the body fat standards. If placed into the same fitness zone, students would receive similar information regardless of whether they are assessed with body fat or BMI.

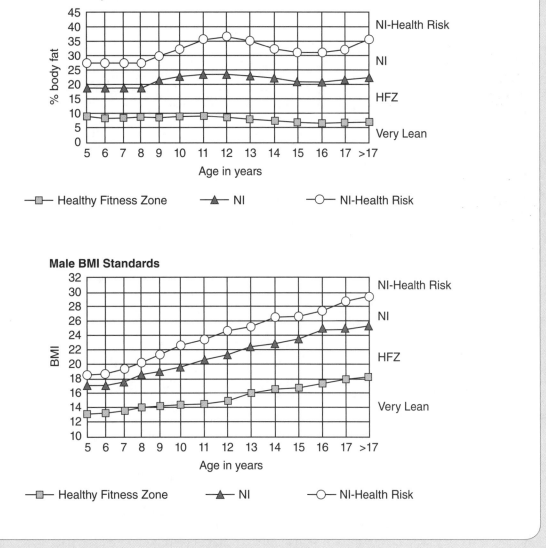

Male Body Fat Standards

Male BMI Standards

(continued)

Overview of the *FITNESSGRAM* Body Composition Standards (*continued*)

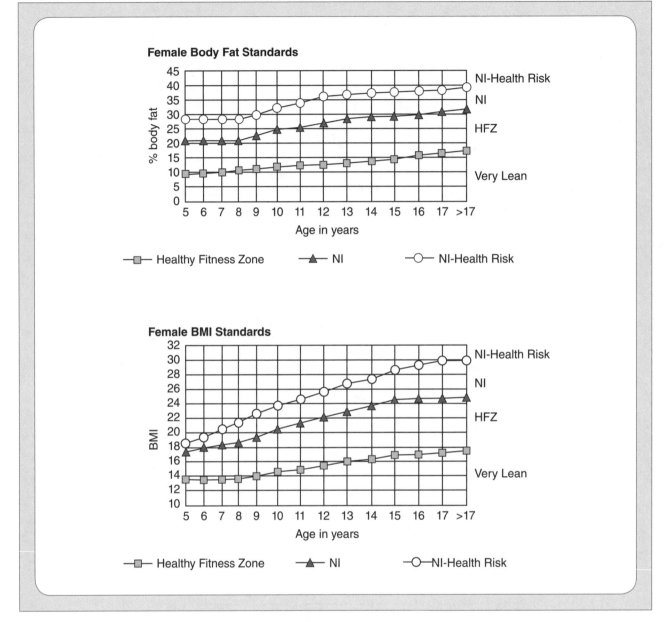

Skinfold Measurements

This section provides information on measuring skinfolds, including suggestions on performing the measurements.

Equipment

A skinfold caliper is necessary for performing this measurement. The caliper measures the thickness of a double layer of subcutaneous fat and skin at different parts of the body. The cost of calipers ranges from $5 to $200. Appendix A on page 85 lists a source for calipers, but it is important to know that training and practice are more important than the quality of the caliper for body composition assessment.

Testing Procedures

There are multiple procedures for skinfold testing. The *FITNESSGRAM* protocol involves collecting measurements from the triceps and calf. These sites have been chosen for *FITNESSGRAM* because they are easily measured and highly correlated with

(*continued*)

total body fatness. (An additional measure from the abdominal site is used for college students.) Following are details on the location of each of the sites as well as specific measurement tips.

- Triceps: The triceps skinfold is measured on the back of the right arm over the triceps muscle, midway between the elbow and the acromion process of the scapula (photo 6.1). Using a piece of string to find the midpoint is a good suggestion. The skinfold site should be vertical. Pinching the fold slightly above the midpoint will ensure that the fold is measured on the midpoint (photos 6.2 and 6.3).

- Calf: The calf skinfold is measured on the inside of the right leg at the level of maximal girth. The right foot is flat on an elevated surface with the knee flexed at a 90-degree angle (photo 6.4). Grasp the vertical skinfold just above the level of maximal girth (photo 6.5) and take the measurement below the grasp.

- Abdomen (college students only): For college students, the formula for calculating percent body fat includes the abdominal skinfold measurement in addition to the triceps and calf skinfolds. The abdominal skinfold is measured at a site 3 centimeters to the side of the midpoint of the umbilicus and 1 centimeter below it (photo 6.6). The skinfold is horizontal and should be measured on the right side of the body (photo 6.7) while the person relaxes the abdominal wall as much as possible.

For accurate information from skinfolds, it is important to use standardized techniques and to conduct assessments as consistently as possible. The following tips are recommended for accurate skinfold measurements:

- Measure skinfolds on the person's right side.
- Instruct the student to relax the arm or leg being measured.
- Firmly grasp the skinfold between the thumb and forefinger and lift it away from the other body tissue. The grasp should not be so firm as to be painful.
- Place the caliper half an inch (~1.25 cm) below the pinch site.
- Be sure the caliper is in the middle of the fold.
- The recommended procedure is to do one measurement at each site before doing the second measurement at each site and finally the third set of measurements.

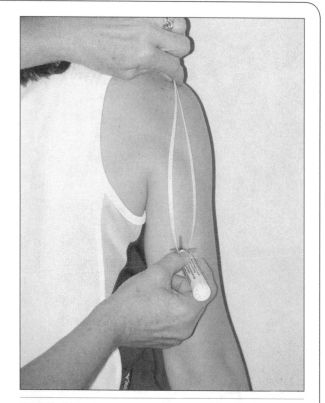

PHOTO 6.1   Locating the triceps skinfold site.

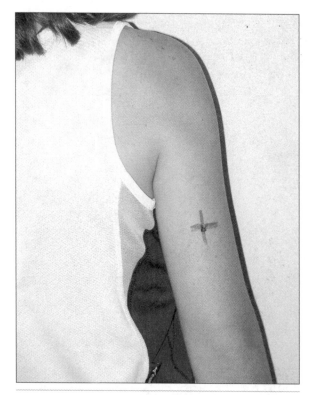

PHOTO 6.2   Site of the triceps skinfold.

(continued)

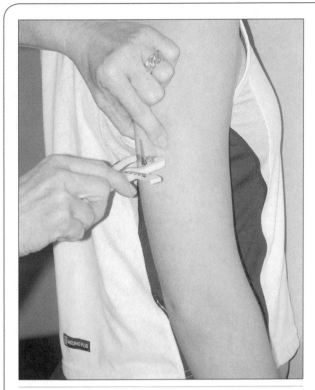

PHOTO 6.3 Triceps skinfold measurement.

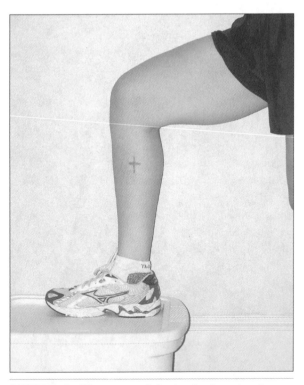

PHOTO 6.4 Placement of the leg for locating the calf skinfold site.

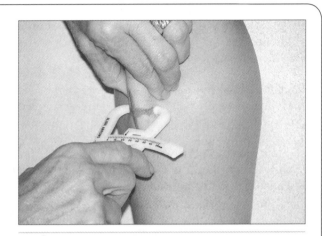

PHOTO 6.5 Calf skinfold measurement.

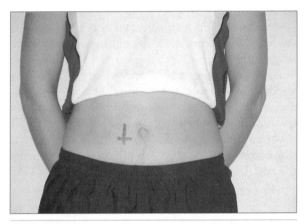

PHOTO 6.6 Site of abdominal skinfold.

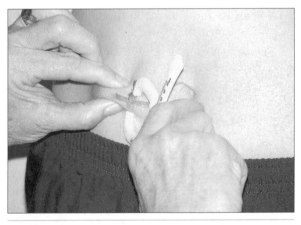

PHOTO 6.7 Abdominal skinfold measurement.

(*continued*)

Skinfold Measurements (continued)

Scoring

The skinfold procedure requires accurate estimates of skinfold thicknesses (measured in millimeters) as shown on the caliper. Each measurement should be taken three times, and the recorded score should be the median (middle) value of the three scores. For example, if the readings were 7.0, 9.0, and 8.0, the score would be recorded as 8.0 millimeters. Each reading should be recorded to the nearest .5 millimeter. For teachers not using the computer software, a percent fatness chart is provided in appendix B on pages 101 and 102 and is also available on the enclosed DVD—access the PDFs titled "Body Comp Conversion_Girls" and "Body Comp Conversion_Boys." *FITNESSGRAM* uses the formula developed by Slaughter and Lohman to calculate percent body fat (Slaughter et al., 1988).

Body Mass Index

The BMI provides an indication of the appropriateness of a child's weight relative to height. Body mass index is determined by the following formula: $BMI = weight (kg) / height^2 (m)$. An example is provided to demonstrate how weight and height interact to influence the BMI score. A student weighing 100 pounds (45.36 kg) who is 5 feet (1.52 m) tall would have a BMI of 19.6. Another student of the same weight but 5 feet 2 inches (1.57 m) tall would have a BMI of 18.3. The same weight is more appropriate for the slightly taller person, so the BMI is slightly lower.

Height and weight measures can be entered into the software in pounds and inches, but they are converted to metric units by the computer to calculate BMI—pounds to kilograms and feet to meters. This section describes how to collect height and weight data and how the results can be interpreted.

Equipment

To collect information about BMI, it is important to obtain accurate measures of height and weight. A stadiometer is recommended for obtaining accurate measurements of height. The use of a tape measure attached to a wall will not be as accurate. For weight, a high-quality digital scale is recommended. Portable stadiometers and digital scales are available for reasonable prices and are a worthwhile investment.

Testing Procedures

To obtain accurate data on height and weight, it is important to measure children without their shoes on. Shoes can be heavy and also can increase a person's height. Therefore, use this procedure for all measurements. In measuring height and weight, you are encouraged to drop fractions of an inch or a pound and use the lower whole number. For example, a height of 5 feet 5.5 inches would be recorded as 5 feet 5 inches, and a weight of 112.5 pounds would be recorded as 112 pounds.

Scoring

The height and weight values are entered into the software, and a BMI is automatically calculated. The general values defining overweight in adults is a value less than 25 (for both males and females). However, boys and girls have BMI values that are very different due to the dramatic changes in growth and development that occur with age. Therefore, age and sex-specific values of BMI are used to assess weight status for youth. Recommended BMI scores are listed in chapter 9.

A score that is classified as Needs Improvement generally indicates that a child weighs too much for his or her height. Body mass index is not the recommended procedure for determining body composition because it does not estimate the percent of fat. It merely provides information on the appropriateness of the weight relative to the height. For children found to be too heavy for their height, a skinfold test would clarify whether the weight is due to excess fat.

Portable Bioelectric Impedance Analyzers

A number of portable bioelectric impedance analyzer (BIA) devices are now commercially available at a price that is reasonable for most physical education programs (<$100). These devices estimate body composition by measuring the body's resistance to current flow. A body with more muscle will also have more total body water (and therefore have low resistance to current flow). A body with more fat will have less total body water and greater resistance to current flow. One type of device requires participants to stand on an instrument resembling a bathroom scale while barefoot. Another type of device uses a handgrip system that has participants squeeze handles while extending the arms.

Preliminary results with these devices suggest that they provide similar accuracy of classification and estimates of body composition as skinfold calipers provide. Because these devices can produce estimates of body composition faster than a skinfold test and do not require specific skill or experience, they may provide a useful alternative to skinfold testing in some schools. The procedure is also less invasive than skinfold testing and may be better accepted in some districts that have specific policies against the use of skinfold calipers.

Additional Recommendations

Suggestions for Test Administration

- Body composition testing should be conducted in a setting that provides each child with privacy.

- Interpretation of the measurements may be given in a group setting as long as individual results are not identified.

- Whenever possible, the same tester should conduct the measurements to ensure consistency.

- Measuring should be practiced, and repeat measurements are recommended occasionally for ensuring accuracy. Once familiar with the methods, testers can generally find agreement within 10%.

Learning to Do Skinfold Measurements

Using video training and participating in workshops are excellent ways to learn skinfold measurements. The video *Practical Body Composition Video* illustrates the procedures described in this manual. Appendix A contains information on obtaining this video.

CHAPTER 7

MUSCULAR STRENGTH, ENDURANCE, AND FLEXIBILITY

Tests of muscular strength, muscular endurance, and flexibility have been combined into one broad fitness category because the primary consideration is determining the functional health status of the musculoskeletal system. It is equally important to have strong muscles that can work forcefully and over a period of time and to be flexible enough to have a full range of motion at the joint. Musculoskeletal injuries are often the result of muscle imbalance at a specific joint; the muscles on one side may be much stronger than the opposing muscles or may not be flexible enough to allow complete motion or sudden motion to occur.

It is important to remember that the specificity of training bears directly on the development of musculoskeletal strength, endurance, and flexibility. The movements included in these test items are only a sampling of the many ways in which the body is required to move and adjust during physical activity.

The upper body and the abdominal/trunk region have been selected as areas for testing because of their perceived relationship to activities of daily living, correct posture, and the development/maintenance of a healthy, well-functioning back.

The goals for a healthy back include proper alignment of the vertebrae and pelvis without excessive disc pressure and the ability of the pelvis to rotate forward and backward without strain on the muscles or connective tissue. To accomplish these goals an individual must have sufficient, but not excessive, flexibility of the low back, hamstring, and hip flexor muscles and strong, fatigue-resistant, abdominal and trunk extensor muscles. Although most students will be able to achieve the criterion standards for one or two of the included test items, it is important to educate them regarding the importance of muscular strength, muscular endurance, and flexibility in preventing problems as adults. It is especially important to make students aware of correct postural alignment and body mechanics in the event that they are developing scoliosis, which is a problem for teenage youth. The school nurse, a local physician, or a physical therapist is a good source of information about scoliosis.

Need Additional Information?

For additional information on the reliability and validity of the different musculoskeletal fitness tests and derivation of the *FITNESSGRAM* Healthy Fitness Zone criteria, visit the *FITNESSGRAM Reference Guide*. The *Guide* is available on the enclosed DVD or online at the *FITNESSGRAM* Web site, www.fitnessgram.net (go to the *Reference Guide* section). Read the chapter "Muscular Strength, Endurance, and Flexibility Assessments" by Plowman.

Abdominal Strength and Endurance

Strength and endurance of the abdominal muscles are important in promoting good posture and correct pelvic alignment. The latter is particularly important in the maintenance of low back health. In testing and training the muscles of this region, it is difficult to isolate the abdominal muscles. The modified sit-up, which is used in many fitness tests, involves the action of the hip flexor muscles in addition to the abdominal muscles. The curl-up assessment used in *FITNESSGRAM* is a safer and more effective test since it does not involve the assistance of the hip flexor muscles and minimizes compression in the spine, when compared to a full sit-up with the feet held. The protocol has been adapted from a version reported by Massicote (1990).

Curl-Up

⇨ *Recommended*

This section provides information on the curl-up assessment used in *FITNESSGRAM*. The curl-up with knees flexed and feet unanchored has been selected because individually these elements have been shown to a) decrease movement of the fifth lumbar vertebra over the sacral vertebrae, b) minimize the activation of the hip flexors, c) increase the activation of the external and internal obliques and transverse abdominals, and d) maximize abdominal muscle activation of the lower and upper rectus abdominals relative to disc compression (load) when compared with a variety of sit-ups.

Few results are available on the consistency and accuracy of the curl-up. Reliability is higher for college students than for children but the values are acceptable for this type of assessment. Determination of validity has been hampered by the lack of an established criterion measure. Anatomical analysis and electromyographical documentation provide the primary support for the use of the curl-up test to determine abdominal strength and endurance.

Test Objective

To complete as many curl-ups as possible up to a maximum of 75 at a specified pace.

Equipment and Facilities

Gym mats and a measuring strip for every two students are needed. The measuring strip may be made of cardboard, rubber, smooth wood, or any similar thin, flat material and should be 30 to 35 inches long. Two widths of measuring strip may be needed. The narrower strip should be 3 inches wide and is used to test 5- to 9-year-olds; for older students the strip should be 4.5 inches wide. Other methods of measuring distance such as using tape strips and pencils are suggested in appendix A.

Test Instructions

Allow students to select a partner. Partner A will perform the curl-ups while partner B counts and watches for form errors.

Partner A lies in a supine position on the mat, knees bent at an angle of approximately 140°, feet flat on the floor, legs slightly apart, arms straight and parallel to the trunk with palms of hands resting on the mat. The fingers are stretched out and the head is in contact with the mat. Make sure students have extended their feet as far as possible from the buttocks while still allowing feet to remain flat on floor. The closer the feet are positioned in relation to the buttocks, the more difficult the movement.

After partner A has assumed the correct position on the mat, partner B places a measuring strip on the mat under partner A's legs so that partner A's fingertips are just resting on the nearest edge of the measuring strip (photo 7.1). Partner B then kneels down at partner A's head in a position to count curl-ups and watch for form breaks. Partner B places a piece of paper under partner A's head. The paper will assist partner B in judging if partner A's head touches down on each repetition (photo 7.2). The observer should watch for the paper to crinkle each time partner A touches it with his or her head.

Before beginning the curl-up, it is a good practice for partner B to pull on partner A's hands to ensure that the shoulders are relaxed and in a normal resting position. If partner A is allowed to hunch

(continued)

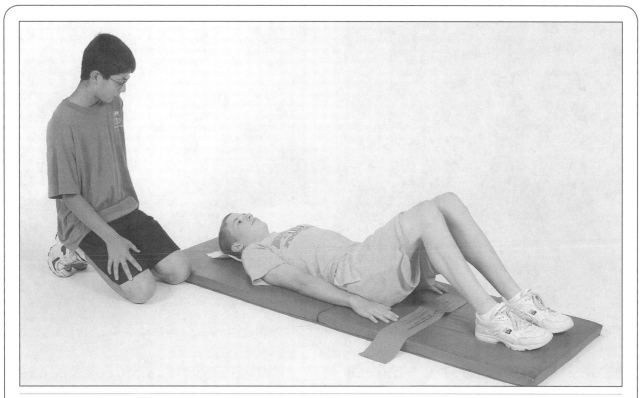

PHOTO 7.1   Starting position for the curl-up test.

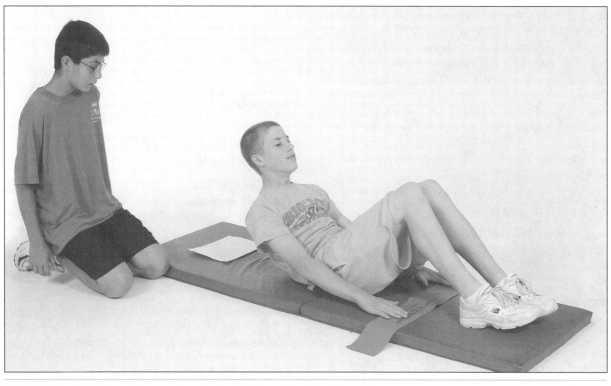

PHOTO 7.2   Position of the student in the "up" position for the curl-up test.

(continued)

Curl-Up *(continued)*

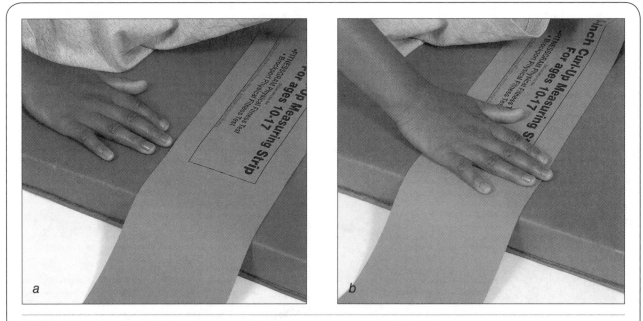

PHOTO 7.3   Close-up of the fingertips sliding: *(a)* starting position and *(b)* ending position.

the shoulders before beginning the test, he or she may be able to get the fingertips to the other side of the testing strip by merely moving the arms and shoulders up and down. Keeping heels in contact with the mat, partner A curls up slowly, sliding fingers across the measuring strip until fingertips reach the other side (photo 7.3, *a* and *b*); then partner A curls back down until his or her head touches the piece of paper on the mat. Movement should be slow and gauged to the specified cadence of about 20 curl-ups per minute (1 curl every 3 seconds). The teacher should call a cadence or use a prerecorded cadence. A recorded cadence may be found on the PACER music tape or CD. Partner A continues without pausing until he or she can no longer continue or has completed 75 curl-ups.

When to Stop

Students are stopped after completing 75 curl-ups, when the **second** form correction is made, or when they can no longer continue.

Form Corrections

- Heels must remain in contact with the mat.
- Head must return to the mat on each repetition.
- Pauses and rest periods are not allowed. The movement should be continuous and with the cadence.

- Fingertips must touch the far side of the measuring strip.

Scoring

The score is the number of curl-ups performed. Curl-ups should be counted when the student's head returns to the mat. For ease in administration, it is permissible to count the first incorrect curl-up. It is important to be consistent with all of the students and classes when determining whether or not you will count the first incorrect curl-up.

Suggestions for Test Administration

- The student being tested should reposition if the body moves so that the head does not contact the mat at the appropriate spot or if the measuring strip is out of position.

- Movement should start with a flattening of the lower back followed by a slow curling of the upper spine.

- The hands should slide across the measuring strip until the fingertips reach the opposite side (3 or 4.5 inches) and then return to the supine position. The movement is completed when the back of the head touches the paper placed on mat.

(continued)

Curl-Up *(continued)*

- The cadence will encourage a steady, continuous movement done in the correct form.

- Students should not forcibly "reach" with their arms and hands but simply let the arms passively move along the floor in response to the action of the trunk and shoulders. Any jerking, kipping, or reaching motion will cause the students to constantly move out of position. When students first begin to use this test item, many will want to "reach" with their arms and hands, especially if they have previously done a timed sit-up test.

- This curl-up protocol is quite different from the one-minute sit-up. **Students will need to learn how to correctly perform this curl-up movement and be allowed time to practice.**

Trunk Extensor Strength and Flexibility

A test of trunk extensor strength and flexibility is included in *FITNESSGRAM* because of its relationship to low back health, especially proper vertebral alignment. Musculoskeletal fitness of the abdominal muscles, hamstrings, and back extensors works in concert to maintain posture and helps maintain low back health. The item is included in the assessment in part because of the educational value of simply doing the assessment. Students will learn that trunk extensor strength and flexibility is an important aspect of maintaining a healthy back.

Trunk Lift

⇨ *Recommended*

It is important that attention be given to performance technique during this test. The movement should be performed in a slow and controlled manner. The maximum score on this test is 12 inches. While some flexibility is important, it is not advisable (or safe) to encourage hyperextension.

Test-retest studies of the trunk extension test (done without limiting the lift to 12 inches) have reported high reliability in high school and college aged students. There are no data on the consistency results for younger children.

Research results have shown that isokinetic trunk endurance, torso length, body weight, passive trunk extension, trunk extension endurance, trunk strength, and flexibility all contribute to performance of the trunk lift. However, a single repetition, partially body weight limited, restricted range item, this test is a minimal assessment of the components of trunk strength and flexibility. Most school-aged individuals will pass this test easily.

Test Objective

To lift the upper body off the floor using the muscles of the back and hold the position to allow for the measurement.

Equipment and Facilities

Gym mats and a measuring device are required to administer this test. A yardstick or 15-inch ruler is preferred; however a 12-inch ruler could be used if care is taken to make certain that the ruler is not placed directly under the student's chin. If students are measuring each other, the "rulers" should be made of some pliable material such as poster board. It is helpful to mark the 6-, 9-, and 12-inch marks with tape. Rope cut to 12 inches with the inch marks taped can also be used as a measuring device.

Test Instructions

The student being tested lies on the mat in a prone position (facedown). Toes are pointed and hands are placed under the thighs. Place a coin or other marker on the floor in line with the student's eyes. During the movement, the student's focus should not move from the coin or marker. The student lifts the upper body off the floor, in a very slow and controlled manner, to a maximum height of 12 inches (photos 7.4, 7.5, and 7.6). The head should be maintained in a neutral (straight) alignment with the spine. The position is held long enough to allow the tester to place the ruler on the floor in front of the student and determine the distance from the floor to the student's chin. The ruler should be

(continued)

PHOTO 7.4   Starting position for the trunk lift.

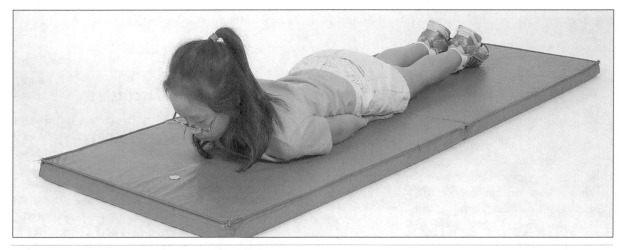

PHOTO 7.5   Student in the "up" position for the trunk lift.

PHOTO 7.6   Measurement of trunk lift.

(*continued*)

Trunk Lift *(continued)*

placed at least an inch to the front of the student's chin and not directly under the chin. Once the measurement has been made, the student returns to the starting position in a controlled manner. Allow two trials, recording the highest score.

Scoring

The score is recorded in inches. Distances above 12 inches should be recorded as 12 inches.

Suggestions for Test Administration

- Do not allow students to do ballistic, bouncing movements.

- Do not encourage students to raise higher than 12 inches. The Healthy Fitness Zone ends at 12 inches, and scores beyond 12 inches will not be accepted by the computer. Excessive arching of the back may cause compression of the spinal discs.

- Maintaining focus on the spot on the floor should assist in maintaining the head in a neutral position.

- Partner B should make the reading at eye level and, therefore, should assume a squat or lying down position.

Upper Body Strength and Endurance

Strength and endurance of the muscles in the upper body are important in activities of daily living, maintaining functional health and promoting good posture. The role of upper body strength in maintaining functionality becomes more evident as a person ages. It is important that children and youth learn the importance of upper body strength and endurance as well as methods to use in developing and maintaining this area of fitness. The 90° push-up is the recommended test item. This 90° push-up has been adapted from assessments reported by Massicote (1990). Alternatives include the modified pull-up, pull-up (not an option with 8.x or 9.x software), and flexed arm hang. It should be noted that although all of these items are intended to measure upper arm and shoulder girdle strength and endurance, they do not all involve the same muscle groups to the same extent and handling body weight is more of a factor in some than others.

90° Push-Up

⇨ *Recommended*

The 90° push-up to an elbow angle of 90° is the recommended test for upper body strength and endurance. Test administration requires little or no equipment; multiple students may be tested at one time; and few zero scores result. This test also teaches students an activity that can be used throughout life as a conditioning activity as well as in self-testing.

The 90° push-up has generally been shown to produce consistent scores but reliability depends on how it is administered. Lower values have been reported for elementary aged students using partners to count the repetitions. Objectivity, or the ability of different observers to attain the same results, is a factor in this item because of the necessity of judging the 90° angle. Scores from student partners are consistently higher than adult counts because students tend to simply count each attempted 90° push-up and not evaluate whether it was done correctly. As with several of the other neuromuscular fitness items, determining the accuracy of the 90° push-up as a test of upper body strength and endurance is made difficult by the lack of an agreed upon criterion measure. Specific validation data are available for the 90° push-up in only two studies conducted on college age students. Validity coefficients against a 1-RM bench press were the highest when the criterion test was the number of repetitions (endurance) at an absolute, but sex-specific, load.

Before test day, students should be allowed to practice doing 90° push-ups and watching their partner do them. Teachers should make a concerted effort during these practice sessions to correct students who are not achieving the 90° angle. In this manner all students will gain greater skill in knowing what 90° "feels like" and "looks like."

(continued)

90° Push-Up *(continued)*

Test Objective

To complete as many 90° push-ups as possible at a rhythmic pace. This test item is used for males and females.

Equipment and Facilities

The only equipment necessary is an audiotape with the recorded cadence. The correct cadence is 20 90° push-ups per minute (1 90° push-up every 3 seconds). The PACER test CD or tape contains a recorded 90° push-up cadence. The 90° push-up may be performed on a mat. Squares of cardboard or anything else that has a 90° angle may assist students in judging 90°.

Test Instructions

The students should be paired; one will perform the test while the other counts 90° push-ups and watches to see that the student being tested bends the elbow to 90° with the upper arm parallel to the floor.

The student being tested assumes a prone position on the mat with hands placed under or slightly wider than the shoulders, fingers stretched out, legs straight and slightly apart, and toes tucked under. The student pushes up off the mat with the arms until arms are straight, keeping the legs and back straight. The back should be kept in a straight line from head to toes throughout the test (photo 7.7).

The student then lowers the body using the arms until the elbows bend at a 90° angle and the upper arms are parallel to the floor (photo 7.8). This movement is repeated as many times as possible. The student should push up and continue the movement until the arms are straight on each repetition. The rhythm should be approximately 20 90° push-ups per minute or 1 90° push-up every 3 seconds.

When to Stop

Students are stopped when the second form correction (mistake) is made. Only one form correction is allowed.

Form Corrections

- Stopping to rest or not maintaining a rhythmic pace
- Not achieving a 90° angle with the elbow on each repetition
- Not maintaining correct body position with a straight back
- Not extending arms fully

Scoring

The score is the number of 90° push-ups performed. For ease in administration, it is permissible to count the first incorrect 90° push-up. It is important to be consistent with all of the students and classes

PHOTO 7.7 Starting position for the 90° push-up test.

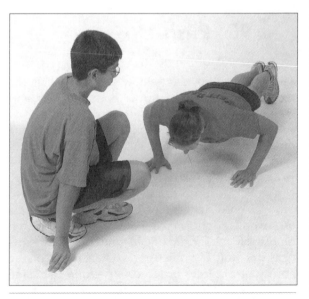

PHOTO 7.8 Student in the "down" position for the 90° push-up test.

(continued)

90° Push-Up (*continued*)

when determining if you will count the first incorrect push-up.

Suggestions for Test Administration

■ Test should be terminated if the student appears to be in extreme discomfort or pain.

■ Cadence should be called or played on a prerecorded tape or CD.

■ Males and females follow the same protocol.

■ Find a short cone or other piece of pliable equipment that could be placed under the student's chest. The student must lower to the equipment in order for the 90° push-up to count. The size and height of the equipment that is used may vary depending on the age and size of your students.

■ It may be helpful to make a recording with a voice-over that counts the number of 90° push-ups for the students (record the teacher counting over the cadence CD).

Modified Pull-Up

⇨ *Alternative*

The modified pull-up shares the advantage of few zero scores and a wide range of scores with the 90° push-up. However, it does not, as commonly believed, negate the effect of body composition/weight on upper body performance. For schools with access to equipment , and desiring to test students individually, the modified pull-up is a very good test item to use.

The modified pull-up has been found to be a reliable test in primary, middle, and high school students. The modified pull-up has not been validated against a criterion measure but it has logical validity based on anatomical principles.

Test Objective

To successfully complete as many modified pull-ups as possible.

Equipment and Facilities

A modified pull-up stand, elastic band, pencil, and score sheet are necessary for administering this test. It is suggested that this assessment be performed on a mat or other soft surface. See appendix A on page 87 for instructions for constructing the modified pull-up stand.

Test Instructions

Position the student on his or her back with shoulders directly under a bar that has been set 1 to 2 inches above the student's reach. Place an elastic band 7 to 8 inches below and parallel to the bar.

The student grasps the bar with an overhand grip (palms away from body). The pull-up begins in this "down" position with arms and legs straight, buttocks off the floor, and only the heels touching the floor (photo 7.9). The student then pulls up until the chin is above the elastic band

PHOTO 7.9 Starting position for the modified pull-up test.

(*continued*)

Modified Pull-Up *(continued)*

PHOTO 7.10 Student in the "up" position for the modified pull-up test.

(photo 7.10). The student then lowers the body to the "down" position. Movement continues in a rhythmic manner.

When to Stop

Students are stopped when the second form correction is made. There is no time limit, but movement should be rhythmical and continuous. Students should not stop and rest.

Form Corrections

- Stopping to rest or not maintaining a rhythmic pace
- Not lifting the chin above the elastic band
- Not maintaining straight body position with only heels in contact with the floor
- Not fully extending arms in the down position

Scoring

The score is the number of pull-ups performed. For ease in administration it is permissible to count the first incorrect pull-up. It is important to be consistent with all of the students and classes when determining if you will count the first incorrect pull-up.

Suggestions for Test Administration

- The test is terminated if the student experiences extreme discomfort or pain.
- Males and females follow the same protocol.

Pull-Up

➪ *Alternative (Only an option for 6.0 users; not an option with 8.x or 9.x software)*

The pull-up test is not the recommended test item for the vast majority of students because many are unable to perform even one pull-up. **This test item should not be used for students who cannot perform one repetition.** However, for those students who are able to perform correct pull-ups this is an item that can be used throughout life as a conditioning activity as well as a self-test.

Reliability of the pull-up has been shown to be acceptable for elementary boys and girls. Attempts at validating the pull-up as a measure of strength against a 1-RM latissimus pull-down have generally not been successful. Validity is equally poor when evaluated against a percentage (50-60% typically) of a 1-RM latissimus pull-down as an indication of upper arm and shoulder girdle endurance, ranging from only .09 to .25. As with the other measures of upper body strength and endurance, at least part of the problem may be the lack of a real criterion test.

Test Objective

To correctly complete as many pull-ups as possible.

(continued)

Pull-Up *(continued)*

Equipment and Facilities

This test uses a horizontal bar at a height that allows the student to hang with arms fully extended and feet clear of the floor. A doorway gym bar may be used.

Test Instructions

The student assumes a hanging position on the bar with an overhand grasp (palms facing away from the body) as shown in photo 7.11. Shorter students may be lifted into the starting position. The student uses the arms to pull the body up until the chin is above the bar (photo 7.12) and then lowers the body again into the full hanging position. The exercise is repeated as many times as possible. There is no time limit.

When to Stop

Students are stopped when the second form correction (mistake) is made.

Form Corrections

■ The body should not swing during the movement. If the student starts to swing, the teacher or assistant should hold an arm in front of the student's thighs to prevent swinging. Swinging of the body or excessive movement is a form correction.

■ The pull-up must be performed smoothly with no kicking or jerking. Forceful bending of the knees or kipping of the body is not permitted.

■ To be counted, a pull-up must result in the chin being lifted over the bar, and the student must return to the full hanging position with elbows fully extended.

PHOTO 7.11   Starting position for the pull-up test.

PHOTO 7.12   Student in the "up" position for the pull-up test.

(continued)

Pull-Up *(continued)*

Scoring

The score is the number of complete pull-ups performed. For ease in administration, it is permissible to count the first incorrect pull-up. It is important to be consistent with all of the students and classes when determining if you will count the first incorrect pull-up. **The computer software will not accept a score of 0 for this test item.**

Suggestions for Test Administration

- A stack of mats off to the side of the hanging bar may be used to help students grasp the bar.

- The teacher may help the student into position and make certain that the body is in the proper position before beginning the test.

Flexed Arm Hang

⇨ *Alternative*

A third alternative to the recommended 90° push-up is the flexed arm hang. The flexed arm hang is a static test of upper body strength and endurance.

Consistency in times for the flexed arm hang has been shown to be acceptable in both 9- and 10-year-olds and college aged students. Two studies, which have attempted to validate the flexed arm hang against the 1-RM arm curl for endurance have shown weak correlations. Thus, only anatomical logic validates this item, as with most of the other upper body tests.

PHOTO 7.13 Starting position for the flexed arm hang test.

PHOTO 7.14 Student in the "up" position for the flexed arm hang test.

(continued)

Flexed Arm Hang (*continued*)

Test Objective

To hang with the chin above the bar as long as possible.

Equipment and Facilities

A horizontal bar, chair or stool (optional), and stopwatch are required to administer this test item.

Test Instructions

The student grasps the bar with an overhand grip (palms facing away). With the assistance of one or more spotters, the student raises the body off the floor to a position in which the chin is above the bar, elbows are flexed, and the chest is close to the bar (photos 7.13 and 7.14). A stopwatch is started as soon as the student takes this position. The position is held as long as possible.

When to Stop

The watch is stopped when one of the following occurs:

- The student's chin touches the bar.
- The student tilts his or her head back to keep the chin above the bar.
- The student's chin falls below the bar.

Scoring

The score is the number of seconds for which the student is able to maintain the correct hanging position.

Suggestions for Test Administration

- The body must not swing during the test. If the student starts to swing, the teacher or assistant should hold an extended arm across the front of the thighs to prevent the swinging motion.

- Only one trial is permitted unless the teacher believes that the pupil has not had a fair opportunity to perform.

Flexibility

Maintaining adequate joint flexibility is important to functional health. However, for young people, decreased flexibility is generally not a problem. Many of your students will easily pass the flexibility item; therefore, the flexibility item has been made optional. If you decide not to administer the flexibility test, remember that you should teach students about flexibility and inform them that maintaining flexibility and range of motion will be important as they age.

Back-Saver Sit and Reach

⇨ *Optional*

The back-saver sit and reach is very similar to the traditional sit and reach except that the measurement is performed on one side at a time. By testing one leg at a time a determination can be made of any asymmetry in hamstring flexibility, and hyperextension of both knees is avoided. The sit and reach measures predominantly the flexibility of the hamstring muscles. Normal hamstring flexibility allows rotation of the pelvis in forward bending movements and posterior tilting of the pelvis for proper sitting.

The back-saver sit and reach has been shown to provide extremely consistent scores when administered under standardized conditions. The back-saver sit and reach has also been shown to be a reasonably accurate measure of hamstring flexibility. When compared with criterion measures of hamstring flexibility, the correlations for both right and left legs have been moderate to high. Conversely, the back-saver sit and reach has been shown to correlate poorly with criterion tests

(continued)

Back-Saver Sit and Reach (*continued*)

of low back flexibility. Therefore, the back-saver sit and reach cannot be considered a valid measure of low back flexibility and should not be interpreted as such.

Test Objective

To be able to reach the specified distance on the right and left sides of the body. The distance required to achieve Healthy Fitness Zone is adjusted for age and gender and is specified in tables 9.1 and 9.2 on pages 65 and 66.

Equipment and Facilities

This assessment requires a sturdy box approximately 12 inches high. A measuring scale is placed on top of the box with the 9-inch mark parallel to the face of the box against which the student's foot will rest. The "zero" end of the ruler is nearest the student. Instructions for construction of a special measuring apparatus are contained in appendix A on page 88. However, a wooden box and yardstick will suffice. Tape the yardstick to the top of the box with the 9-inch mark at the nearest edge of the box. The "zero" end of the yardstick is nearest the student.

Test Instructions

The student removes his or her shoes and sits down at the test apparatus. One leg is fully extended with the foot flat against the face of the box. The other knee is bent with the sole of the foot flat on the floor. The instep is placed in line with, and 2 to 3 inches to the side of, the straight knee. The arms are extended forward over the measuring scale with the hands placed one on top of the other (photo 7.15). With palms down, the student reaches directly forward (keeping back straight and the head up) with both hands along the scale four times and holds the position of the fourth reach for at least 1 second (photo 7.16). After one side has been measured, the student switches the position of the legs and reaches again. The student may allow the bent knee to move to the side as the body moves

PHOTO 7.15 Starting position for measuring the right side.

PHOTO 7.16 Back-saver sit and reach stretch for the right side.

(*continued*)

Back-Saver Sit and Reach (*continued*)

forward if necessary, but the sole of the foot must remain on the floor.

Scoring

Record the number of inches on each side to the nearest 1/2 inch reached, to a maximum score of 12 inches. Performance is limited to discourage hypermobility. To be in the Healthy Fitness Zone, the student should meet the standard on both the right and the left sides.

Suggestions for Test Administration

- The bent knee moves to the side, allowing the body to move past it, but the sole of the foot must remain on the floor.

- Keep the back straight and the head up during the forward flexion movement.

- The knee of the extended leg should remain straight. Tester may place one hand above the student's knee to help keep the knee straight.

- Hands should reach forward evenly.

- The trial should be repeated if the hands reach unevenly or the knee bends.

- Hips must remain square to the box. Do not allow the student to turn the hip away from the box while reaching.

Shoulder Stretch

⇨ *Optional*

The shoulder stretch is a simple test of upper arm and shoulder girdle flexibility intended to parallel the strength/endurance assessment of that region. If used alternately with the back-saver sit and reach, it may be useful in educating students that flexibility is specific to each joint and that hamstring flexibility neither represents a total body flexibility nor is the only part of the body where flexibility is important.

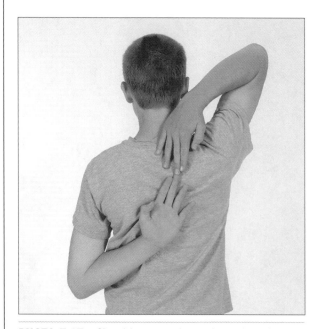

PHOTO 7.17 Shoulder stretch on the right side.

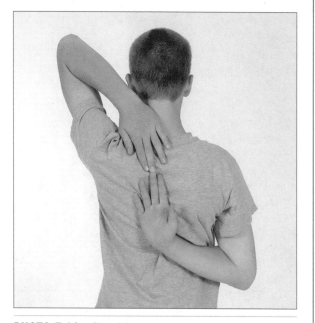

PHOTO 7.18 Shoulder stretch on the left side.

(*continued*)

Shoulder Stretch (*continued*)

Test Objective

To be able to touch the fingertips together behind the back by reaching over the shoulder and under the elbow.

Equipment and Facilities

No equipment is necessary to complete this test item.

Test Description

Allow students to select a partner. The partner judges ability to complete the stretch.

To test the right shoulder, partner A reaches with the right hand over the right shoulder and down the back as if to pull up a zipper or scratch between the shoulder blades. At the same time partner A places the left hand behind the back and reaches up, trying to touch the fingers of the right hand (photo 7.17). Partner B observes whether the fingers touch.

To test the left shoulder, partner A reaches with the left hand over the left shoulder and down the back as if to pull up a zipper or scratch between the shoulder blades. At the same time partner A places the right hand behind the back and reaches up, trying to touch the fingers of the left hand (photo 7.18). Partner B notes whether the fingers touch.

Scoring

If the student is able to touch his or her fingers with the left hand over the shoulder, a "Y" is recorded for the left side; if not, an "N" is recorded. If the student is able to touch the fingers with the right hand over the shoulder, a "Y" is recorded for the right side; otherwise an "N" is recorded. To achieve the Healthy Fitness Zone, a "Y" must be recorded on both the right and left side.

CHAPTER 8

FITNESSGRAM PHYSICAL ACTIVITY QUESTIONS

The physical activity questions were added to the *FITNESSGRAM* software to improve the prescriptive information that is given to the student. Many factors, including heredity, maturation, and body composition, can influence a child's performance on physical fitness tests. Some children may get discouraged if they do not score well on fitness tests despite being active. Alternatively, children may incorrectly believe that they don't need to be active if their fitness levels are in the Healthy Fitness Zone. Through the physical activity assessment in the *FITNESSGRAM* test protocol, students will learn to more directly associate physical activity with physical fitness. The activity assessment also allows for the provision of more personalized information on the *FITNESSGRAM* report. This feedback will reinforce the notion that it is important to be physically active regardless of fitness level.

This chapter describes the physical activity questions and explains how to access and incorporate this part of the assessment into the *FITNESSGRAM* testing protocol. It also provides information on how the responses are used to modify the prescriptive feedback on the *FITNESSGRAM* reports.

Description of Activity Assessment

The assessment includes three brief questions that are based on items from the Youth Risk Behavior Survey—a national surveillance instrument used to track nationwide trends in physical activity. Each question asks the students to report the number of days in a given week on which they performed different forms of physical activity (aerobic, muscular strength and endurance, and flexibility). Table 8.1 shows the wording of the questions.

Administration

Because it may be difficult for young children to accurately recall this information, the activity assessments may not be valid for children from grades K through 4. To increase the validity of the assessment it is recommended that teachers prepare the students ahead of time to answer these questions. Be sure to explain the different types of physical activity (aerobic, muscular strength

TABLE 8.1	*FITNESSGRAM* Physical Activity Questions
Activity area	**Question**
Aerobic	On how many of the past 7 days did you participate in any physical activity for a total of 30 to 60 minutes or more over the course of a day? This includes moderate activities (walking, slow bicycling, or outdoor play) as well as vigorous activities (jogging, active games, or active sports such as basketball, tennis, or soccer). (0, 1, 2, 3, 4, 5, 6, 7 days)
Muscular strength & endurance	On how many of the past 7 days did you do exercises to strengthen or tone your muscles? This includes exercises such as push-ups, sit-ups, or weightlifting. (0, 1, 2, 3, 4, 5, 6, 7 days)
Flexibility	On how many of the past 7 days did you do stretching exercises to loosen up or relax your muscles? This includes exercises such as toe touches, knee bending, or leg stretching. (0, 1, 2, 3, 4, 5, 6, 7 days)

and endurance, and flexibility) and illustrate (with examples) how to count the number of days of activity. This could be done as part of an effort to teach children about how much physical activity they should try to do each week.

Rationale for Completing the Activity Questions

If the child completes the *FITNESSGRAM* physical activity questions, the software incorporates the responses in the evaluative feedback that is provided on the printed *FITNESSGRAM* report card. For example, if a child scores high on fitness but does not appear to be active, he or she receives encouraging information about the need to stay active to maintain his or her fitness. Alternatively, a child who scores low on fitness but appears to be active receives messages encouraging him or her to keep up efforts to be physically active. This information will reinforce to children the importance of being physically active regardless of fitness level. See chapter 9 for more information on interpreting *FITNESSGRAM* reports and for information on how these questions are utilized.

INTERPRETING FITNESSGRAM RESULTS

FITNESSGRAM uses criterion-referenced standards to evaluate fitness performance. These standards have been established to represent a level of fitness that offers some degree of protection against "hypokinetic" diseases (i.e., conditions that result from sedentary living). Performance is classified in two general areas: Healthy Fitness Zone (HFZ) and the "Needs Improvement" zone. Attaining the HFZ for a test indicates that the child has a sufficient fitness level to provide important health benefits. The "Needs Improvement" zone should be interpreted as an indication that the child may be at risk if that level of fitness stays the same over time. For the body composition item, a third Very Low area is designated within the HFZ. Scores falling in this area deserve special attention to determine why the student's score is very low.

This chapter explains how the criterion-referenced standards are established for the different assessments, how maturation and development can influence fitness results, and how to specifically interpret results from the different dimensions of fitness.

Derivation of Criterion-Referenced Standards

To help children understand and interpret these results, it is important to have a basic understanding of how the standards are established. Unlike the percentile-based standards that are used in some fitness batteries, the criterion-referenced standards used in *FITNESSGRAM* are anchored to an outcome that has inherent meaning and importance. Several slight adjustments have been made in the $\dot{V}O_2$max, PACER, and body composition standards since this manual was first published. Detailed information on the derivation of the criterion-referenced standards is available in the *FITNESSGRAM Reference Guide*—see the chapter "Physical Fitness Standards for Children" by Morrow and Falls. The following paragraphs provide brief descriptions of the basis for the standards.

The aerobic fitness standards were established with the use of nationally representative data from the National Health and Nutrition Examination

Survey (NHANES). Data on levels of aerobic capacity (measured with a submaximal clinical exercise test) were associated with the presence of metabolic syndrome, which is a collection of factors that are associated with an increased risk for diabetes and cardiovascular disease (including high triglycerides, high blood pressure, and high levels of circulating insulin). Numerous studies have documented that physical fitness provides protection against health risks, even among overweight youth. Studies have also shown that the benefits of physical fitness may be independent of physical activity. These findings support the importance of evaluating potential health risks that result from low levels of fitness.

The aerobic fitness standards establish three zones based on potential risks for future health problems. The Healthy Fitness Zone was established by determining the level of fitness required for a low risk for future health problems. The Needs Improvement—Health Risk zone defines levels of fitness that indicate potential health risks (current or future risks). Youth between the two zones are classified in an intermediate zone referred to as Needs Improvement.

The aerobic fitness standards are based on estimated aerobic capacity. Each of the primary assessments provides estimates of aerobic capacity, but differences in the tests and the associated prediction equations can lead to differences in fitness classification (depending on what test is used). To minimize misclassification, the PACER test score is equated to a corresponding mile run time to determine estimated aerobic capacity. This improves the classification agreement between the two assessments. Detailed information on the derivation of these standards is available in the chapter Aerobic Capacity Assessments in the *FITNESSGRAM Reference Guide*.

The body composition standards were established with the use of nationally representative data from the National Health and Nutrition Examination Survey (NHANES). Data on body fat were associated with the presence of metabolic syndrome, a collection of risk factors that are associated with an increased risk for diabetes and cardiovascular disease (including high triglycerides, high blood pressure, and high levels of circulating insulin). Evidence from numerous epidemiological studies has documented that body fat levels and associated risk factors track throughout adolescence and into adulthood. It is important to identify youth who may be at increased risk so that preventive or treatment programs can be initiated.

The body composition standards establish three zones based on potential risks for future health problems. The Healthy Fitness Zone was established by determining body fat values that indicate a low risk for potential health problems. The Needs Improvement—Health Risk zone, in contrast, defines levels of body fatness that indicate a clear or substantial risk for future health problems. Youth between the two zones are classified into an intermediate zone referred to as Needs Improvement. These youth are not considered to be at high risk but should be encouraged to keep working to reduce body fat until they reach the Healthy Fitness Zone.

The body fat standards were then equated to corresponding BMI values to ensure good classification agreement between the body fat standards and BMI standards. The two assessments are very different and can't be expected to have perfect agreement. However, the BMI standards can be interpreted in a similar way as the body fat standards described previously. The widely accepted CDC growth charts have proven useful in identifying potential health risk, but these are based on percentile norms rather than health-related standards. These standards are useful for population tracking and surveillance, but the FITNESSGRAM BMI standards provide more specific information about individual health risks. Detailed information on the derivation of the body fat and BMI standards is available in the chapter Body Composition Assessment in the *FITNESSGRAM Reference Guide*.

Criterion-referenced standards for the musculoskeletal fitness assessments are more difficult to establish than those for aerobic capacity or body composition. The reason is that there are few immediate health risks associated with poor musculoskeletal fitness. Lack of strength, muscle endurance, and flexibility may increase the risk of injuries and back problems later in life, but children are not as susceptible to these health problems. This delayed risk makes it more difficult to determine how much fitness is needed to provide important health benefits in this dimension of fitness. The approach for most of these test items is to utilize a "contrasting group methodology" to determine the amount of fitness in each of the tests that would be possible with a reasonable amount of training. By comparing a "trained" group to an "untrained" group it is possible to establish cutpoints that are empirically based and anchored to training responses from exercise rather than health outcomes.

Tables 9.1 and 9.2 provide a list of standards that define the HFZ for each of the assessments. All students should strive to achieve a score that places them inside the HFZ. It is possible for some students to score above the HFZ. *FITNESSGRAM* acknowledges performances above the HFZ but

TABLE 9.1   *FITNESSGRAM*® Standards for Healthy Fitness Zone®

	BOYS											
Age	**Aerobic capacity V̇O₂max (ml/kg/min)**			**Percent body fat**				**Body mass index**			
	PACER, one-mile run, and walk test										
	NI-Health Risk	**NI**	**HFZ**	**Very Lean**	**HFZ**	**NI**	**NI-Health Risk**	**Very Lean**	**HFZ**	**NI**	**NI-Health Risk**
5	Completion of test. Lap count or time standards not recommended.			≤8.8	8.9-18.8	18.9	≥27.0	≤13.8	13.9-16.8	16.9	≥18.1
6				≤8.4	8.5-18.8	18.9	≥27.0	≤13.7	13.8-17.1	17.2	≥18.8
7				≤8.2	8.3-18.8	18.9	≥27.0	≤13.7	13.8-17.6	17.7	≥19.6
8				≤8.3	8.4-18.8	18.9	≥27.0	≤13.9	14.0-18.2	18.3	≥20.6
9				≤8.6	8.7-20.6	20.7	≥30.1	≤14.1	14.2-18.9	19.0	≥21.6
10	≤37.3	37.4-40.1	≥40.2	≤8.8	8.9-22.4	22.5	≥33.2	≤14.4	14.5-19.7	19.8	≥22.7
11	≤37.3	37.4-40.1	≥40.2	≤8.7	8.8-23.6	23.7	≥35.4	≤14.8	14.9-20.5	20.6	≥23.7
12	≤37.6	37.7-40.2	≥40.3	≤8.3	8.4-23.6	23.7	≥35.9	≤15.2	15.3-21.3	21.4	≥24.7
13	≤38.6	38.7-41.0	≥41.1	≤7.7	7.8-22.8	22.9	≥35.0	≤15.7	15.8-22.2	22.3	≥25.6
14	≤39.6	39.7-42.4	≥42.5	≤7.0	7.1-21.3	21.4	≥33.2	≤16.3	16.4-23.0	23.1	≥26.5
15	≤40.6	40.7-43.5	≥43.6	≤6.5	6.6-20.1	20.2	≥31.5	≤16.8	16.9-23.7	23.8	≥27.2
16	≤41.0	41.1-44.0	≥44.1	≤6.4	6.5-20.1	20.2	≥31.6	≤17.4	17.5-24.5	24.6	≥27.9
17	≤41.2	41.3-44.1	≥44.2	≤6.6	6.7-20.9	21.0	≥33.0	≤18.0	18.1-24.9	25.0	≥28.6
>17	≤41.2	41.3-44.2	≥44.3	≤6.9	7.0-22.2	22.3	≥35.1	≤18.5	18.6-24.9	25.0	≥29.3

Age	**Curl-up (no. completed)**	**Trunk lift (inches)**	**90° push-up (no. completed)**	**Modified pull-up (no. completed)**	**Flexed arm hang (seconds)**	**Back-saver sit and reach* (inches)**	**Shoulder stretch**
5	≥2	6-12	≥3	≥2	≥2	8	Healthy Fitness Zone = touching fingertips together behind the back on both the right and left sides.
6	≥2	6-12	≥3	≥2	≥2	8	
7	≥4	6-12	≥4	≥3	≥3	8	
8	≥6	6-12	≥5	≥4	≥3	8	
9	≥9	6-12	≥6	≥5	≥4	8	
10	≥12	9-12	≥7	≥5	≥4	8	
11	≥15	9-12	≥8	≥6	≥6	8	
12	≥18	9-12	≥10	≥7	≥10	8	
13	≥21	9-12	≥12	≥8	≥12	8	
14	≥24	9-12	≥14	≥9	≥15	8	
15	≥24	9-12	≥16	≥10	≥15	8	
16	≥24	9-12	≥18	≥12	≥15	8	
17	≥24	9-12	≥18	≥14	≥15	8	
>17	≥24	9-12	≥18	≥14	≥15	8	

*Test scored Yes/No; must reach this distance on each side to achieve the HFZ.

© 2010 The Cooper Institute, Dallas, Texas.

TABLE 9.2   *FITNESSGRAM*® Standards for Healthy Fitness Zone®

	GIRLS										

Age	Aerobic capacity V̇O₂max (ml/kg/min) PACER, one-mile run, and walk test			Percent body fat				Body mass index			
	NI-Health Risk	NI	HFZ	Very Lean	HFZ	NI	NI-Health Risk	Very Lean	HFZ	NI	NI-High Risk
5	Completion of test. Lap count or time standards not recommended.			≤9.7	9.8-20.8	20.9	≥28.4	≤13.5	13.6-16.8	16.9	≥18.5
6				≤9.8	9.9-20.8	20.9	≥28.4	≤13.4	13.5-17.2	17.3	≥19.2
7				≤10.0	10.1-20.8	20.9	≥28.4	≤13.5	13.6-17.9	18.0	≥20.2
8				≤10.4	10.5-20.8	20.9	≥28.4	≤13.6	13.7-18.6	18.7	≥21.2
9				≤10.9	11.0-22.6	22.7	≥30.8	≤13.9	14.0-19.4	19.5	≥22.4
10	≤37.3	37.4-40.1	≥40.2	≤11.5	11.6-24.3	24.4	≥33.0	≤14.2	14.3-20.3	20.4	≥23.6
11	≤37.3	37.4-40.1	≥40.2	≤12.1	12.2-25.7	25.8	≥34.5	≤14.6	14.7-21.2	21.3	≥24.7
12	≤37.0	37.1-40.0	≥40.1	≤12.6	12.7-26.7	26.8	≥35.5	≤15.1	15.2-22.1	22.2	≥25.8
13	≤36.6	36.7-39.6	≥39.7	≤13.3	13.4-27.7	27.8	≥36.3	≤15.6	15.7-22.9	23.0	≥26.8
14	≤36.3	36.4-39.3	≥39.4	≤13.9	14.0-28.5	28.6	≥36.8	≤16.1	16.2-23.6	23.7	≥27.7
15	≤36.0	36.1-39.0	≥39.1	≤14.5	14.6-29.1	29.2	≥37.1	≤16.6	16.7-24.3	24.4	≥28.5
16	≤35.8	35.9-38.8	≥38.9	≤15.2	15.3-29.7	29.8	≥37.4	≤17.0	17.1-24.8	24.9	≥29.3
17	≤35.7	35.8-38.7	≥38.8	≤15.8	15.9-30.4	30.5	≥37.9	≤17.4	17.5-24.9	25.0	≥30.0
>17	≤35.3	35.4-38.5	≥38.6	≤16.4	16.5-31.3	31.4	≥38.6	≤17.7	17.8-24.9	25.0	≥30.0

Age	Curl-up (no. completed)	Trunk lift (inches)	90° push-up (no. completed)	Modified pull-up (no. completed)	Flexed arm hang (seconds)	Back-saver sit and reach* (inches)	Shoulder stretch
5	≥2	6-12	≥3	≥2	≥2	9	Healthy Fitness Zone = touching fingertips together behind the back on both the right and left sides.
6	≥2	6-12	≥3	≥2	≥2	9	
7	≥4	6-12	≥4	≥3	≥3	9	
8	≥6	6-12	≥5	≥4	≥3	9	
9	≥9	6-12	≥6	≥4	≥4	9	
10	≥12	9-12	≥7	≥4	≥4	9	
11	≥15	9-12	≥7	≥4	≥6	10	
12	≥18	9-12	≥7	≥4	≥7	10	
13	≥18	9-12	≥7	≥4	≥8	10	
14	≥18	9-12	≥7	≥4	≥8	10	
15	≥18	9-12	≥7	≥4	≥8	12	
16	≥18	9-12	≥7	≥4	≥8	12	
17	≥18	9-12	≥7	≥4	≥8	12	
>17	≥18	9-12	≥7	≥4	≥8	12	

*Test scored Yes/No; must reach this distance on each side to achieve the HFZ.

© 2010 The Cooper Institute, Dallas, Texas.

does not recommend this level of performance as an appropriate goal level for all students. However, students who desire to achieve a high level of athletic performance may need to consider setting goals beyond the HFZ. Students, especially younger students, may need assistance in setting realistic goals.

Influence of Body Size and Maturity on Fitness

Body size (height and weight) is to some extent related to physical fitness as measured by a combination of tests. Although there is much variability among individuals, the influence of body size on fitness is especially apparent in two ways:

1. Excess weight associated with fatness tends to have a negative influence on aerobic capacity and on test items in which the body must be lifted or moved (e.g., upper body strength items).

2. Variation in body size associated with maturity can influence fitness around the time of the adolescent growth spurt and sexual maturation. There is considerable variation among individuals in the timing of this maturation period. In adequately nourished children, the timing is largely determined by genetics. Within a given age group of early-adolescent children, there will be great variation in the maturation level.

Changes in body fatness and body size can have major effects on fitness test performance. Boys show a clear growth spurt in muscle mass, strength, power, and endurance and a decrease in subcutaneous fat on the arms and legs. Girls show considerably smaller growth spurts in strength, power, and endurance and tend to accumulate body fat compared to boys. During periods of rapid maturational change, children may experience an increase or decrease in their abilities to perform on certain test items completely independent of their levels of physical activity.

Interpreting Performance on Physical Fitness Assessments

The *FITNESSGRAM* report provides personalized feedback that can help a child (and parent) become more informed about levels of health-related fitness. A sample report is shown in figure 9.1 to highlight some of the features. As is evident in the illustration, the report uses easy-to-read bar charts to indicate fitness levels for each of the completed tests. Comparisons between the past and the current tests allow for some indication of trends over time. Personalized feedback messages that appear in the text blocks help provide individualized feedback to the students. The feedback is processed using internal algorithms in the software that take into account a child's overall fitness profile. Students with favorable scores on the assessments (i.e., those reaching the HFZ) receive congratulatory messages and reminders to maintain their involvement in physical activity. Students with less favorable scores (i.e., those in the "Needs Improvement" zone) receive supportive messages and prescriptive feedback about how to be more active and how to improve their scores.

If scores for more than one assessment in a fitness area are entered in the software, the following guidelines are used to determine which result will be printed:

- If one performance is in the HFZ and the other is not, the better performance will be printed.
- If the performances on all assessments are in the HFZ or are not in the HFZ, the default item will print (PACER, percent body fat, 90° push-up, back-saver sit and reach).

While the assessments in the *FITNESSGRAM* battery have good reliability and validity, the results of the tests should still be used as only rough indicators. A number of factors can influence fitness scores, and most are not within a child's control. As mentioned previously, maturation and development can have a major impact on a child's fitness scores. A child's fitness level and response to training are also determined to a great degree by their genetics. Some children will improve performance more rapidly than others. Some children will be able to perform at a much higher level than others regardless of training levels. Rather than emphasizing a child's fitness scores, it is more important to emphasize involvement in regular physical activity. Good physical fitness levels will not be of much value if they are not maintained through continued involvement in physical activity.

Built-in algorithms within the *FITNESSGRAM* software have been prepared to facilitate this type of instruction. If the *FITNESSGRAM* physical activity questions are completed (see chapter 8), the individualized feedback provided on the *FITNESSGRAM* report will factor in the child's responses to the physical activity questions. This allows a child to receive positive encouragement for being active even if he or she is not in the HFZ.

(FG) FITNESSGRAM®

IN PARTNERSHIP WITH **Play60** THE NFL MOVEMENT FOR AN ACTIVE GENERATION

Joe Jogger
Grade: 5 Age: 12
Washington Middle School
Instructor(s): Mary Jones

	Date	Height	Weight
Current:	5/16/2013	5'1"	123 lbs
Past:	9/17/2012	4'11"	120 lbs

AEROBIC CAPACITY

	Needs Improvement / Health Risk	Healthy Fitness Zone

Aerobic Capacity (VO2 Max)

Current: 41.3
Past: 40.3

Your score for Aerobic Capacity is based on the number of PACER laps. It shows your ability to do activities such as running, cycling, and sports at a high level.

PACER Laps
Current: 26
Past: 20

MUSCLE STRENGTH, ENDURANCE, & FLEXIBILITY

	Needs Improvement	Healthy Fitness Zone

(Abdominal)Curl-Up

Current: 15
Past: 10

(Trunk Extension)Trunk Lift

Current: 10
Past: 9

(Upper Body)Push-Up

Current: 12
Past: 12

(Flexibility)Back-Saver Sit and Reach R,L

Current: 11.00, 11.00
Past: 9.00, 9.00

BODY COMPOSITION

Body Mass Index

Healthy Fitness Zone	Needs Improvement / Health Risk

Current: 23.2
Past: 24.2

Being too lean or too heavy may be a sign of (or lead to) health problems. Body Mass Index may give inaccurate results for very active children.

ACTIVITY

	Number of Days
On how many of the past 7 days did you participate in physical activity for a total of 30-60 minutes, or more, over the course of the day?	4
On how many of the past 7 days did you do exercises to strengthen or tone your muscles?	4
On how many of the past 7 days did you do exercises to loosen up or relax your muscles?	3

MESSAGES

Your aerobic capacity score is in the Healthy Fitness Zone now, but you could be more physically active. To maintain fitness, participate in physical activities that make you breathe hard for at least 60 minutes each day. BMI also affects aerobic capacity.

Your trunk and upper-body strength are both in the Healthy Fitness Zone. To maintain your fitness, be sure that your strength-training activities include exercises for each of these areas. Trunk exercises should be done 3 to 5 days each week. Strength activities for other areas should be done 3 days.

To improve your abdominal strength, be sure that your strength activities include curl-ups. You may need to do more curl-ups each day or do them more days of the week.

Your flexibility is in the Healthy Fitness Zone. To maintain your fitness, stretch slowly 3 or 4 days each week, holding the stretch 20-30 seconds. Don't forget that you need to stretch all areas of the body.

Body composition at this level may need improvement. Healthy body composition and regular physical activity are important for overall good health. Here are some tips to improve body composition:
-Be active for at least 60 minutes every day.
-Limit time spent watching TV or playing video games.
-Eat a healthy diet including fresh fruits and vegetables.
-Limit your calories from foods with solid fats and added sugars and avoid sugary drinks.
If you are usually very active this could be an incorrect result. Ask your parent or teacher for more information.

Healthy Fitness Zone for 12 year-old boys
Aerobic Capacity: >= 40.3 ml/kg/min
Curl-Up: >= 18 repetitions
Trunk Lift: 9-12 inches
Push-Up: >= 10 repetitions
Back-Saver Sit and Reach: At least 8 inches on R & L
Body Mass Index: 15.3 - 21.3

To be healthy and fit it is important to do some physical activity almost every day. Aerobic exercise is good for your heart and body composition. Strength and flexibility exercises are good for your muscles and joints.

Good job! You are doing some aerobic activity and strength and flexibility exercises. Additional vigorous activity would help to promote higher levels of fitness.

This report is for informational purposes and intended only as a guide to raise awareness of fitness and good health. © 2013 The Cooper Institute

FIGURE 9.1 Sample *FITNESSGRAM* computer report.

TABLE 9.3   Conceptual Matrix Used to Integrate Fitness and Activity Results

Fitness results	Physically active?	
	Yes	**No**
Scores in Healthy Fitness Zone	Congratulations. You are in the Healthy Fitness Zone. You are doing regular physical activity and this is keeping you fit.	Congratulations. You are in the Healthy Fitness Zone. To keep fit it is important that you do regular physical activity.
Scores not in Healthy Fitness Zone	Even though your scores were not in the Healthy Fitness Zone, you are doing enough physical activity. Keep up the good work.	Your scores were not in the Healthy Fitness Zone. Try to increase your activity levels to improve your fitness and health.

Conversely, this feedback provides clear indications to other children that it is important to be active even if they are already fit. The conceptual matrix in table 9.3 illustrates the general content of the integrated fitness and activity feedback. Although the actual feedback will be specific for each dimension of fitness (aerobic, musculoskeletal, and body composition) and will be more detailed, this chart illustrates the general concept. The questions are optional but strongly recommended. If children do not complete the questions, then the feedback will be based only on their fitness scores, and this may send the wrong message.

Because the different dimensions of fitness are influenced by different factors, the following sections provide specific information to help summarize how each dimension of fitness should be interpreted and how each can be improved.

Aerobic Capacity

Aerobic capacity indicates the ability of the respiratory, cardiovascular, and muscular systems to take up, transport, and utilize oxygen during exercise and activity. A laboratory measure of $\dot{V}O_2$max is generally the best measure of aerobic capacity. *FITNESSGRAM* output for this area of fitness is now the calculated score for aerobic capacity. This calculated score on aerobic capacity may be used in comparing performance from one test date to another or among different test items. A low score on the aerobic field test may be influenced by many factors:

- Actual aerobic capacity level
- Body composition
- Running and walking efficiency and economy
- Motivation level during the actual testing experience
- Extreme environmental conditions
- Ability to pace on the one-mile run and the walk test
- Genetics and innate ability

Changes in any of these factors may influence the test score.

Aerobic capacity can be improved substantially in an unconditioned person who participates regularly in sustained activities involving large muscle groups. The amount of improvement is related to the beginning level of fitness and to the intensity, duration, and frequency of the training. The major part of the improvement will occur during the first six months. Thereafter, improvement will be much slower. Boys and girls who are overfat may expect an improvement in the aerobic capacity measure with a reduction in body fat.

Changes caused by maturation can influence results on the tests. For boys, aerobic capacity in relation to body weight stays relatively constant during the growing years. For girls, aerobic capacity tends to remain constant between ages 5 and 10 years but decreases after age 10 due to increasing sex-specific essential fat. Running economy, however, also exerts an influence on absolute performance. In boys, for example, one-mile run test scores tend to improve progressively with age, even though $\dot{V}O_2$max expressed relative to body weight tends to remain constant, because running economy improves. In 10- to 12-year-old girls, these field test scores also tend to improve as the result of improved running economy; but between ages 12 and 18, scores tend to remain relatively constant because improved running economy is offset by declining VO$_2$max expressed relative to body weight. The differences in age-related changes in the relation of the one-mile run or PACER test scores to running economy are taken into account when the scores are converted to estimated VO$_2$max by equations in the *FITNESS-GRAM* program software.

Body Composition

Body composition standards have been established for both percent body fat calculated from triceps and calf skinfold measurements (for college students, abdominal skinfold is also included) and for BMI calculated from measurements of weight and height. The HFZ standards fall between the Very Lean category and the Needs Improvement categories. Scores that fall either below or above the HFZ should receive attention, because those students have greater potential than others to develop health problems related to their level of fatness or leanness.

Tables 9.1 and 9.2 indicate the HFZ for both percent fat and BMI as well as the Needs Improvement, Needs Improvement—Health Risk, and the Very Lean categories. Ideally, students should strive to be within the HFZ. A score in the Needs Improvement category indicates that the student is either overfat or the student's weight is too high for his or her height. However, students who are extremely muscular may have a BMI in the Needs Improvement area but may not have excess fat. Students in the Needs Improvement category should work to move into the HFZ because their level of body composition puts them at some risk of developing health problems. Students in the Needs Improvement—Health Risk category must be strongly encouraged to modify their activity and eating behaviors to begin reducing their weight. Students in this Health Risk category have a great possibility of developing health problems now and in the future if their body composition does not change.

When interpreting body composition scores, remember the following:

- Skinfold measurements provide an estimate of body fatness.
- A 3% to 5% error in body fat measurement is associated with the skinfold method.
- Body mass index provides an estimate of the appropriateness of the weight for the height.
- Body mass index may falsely identify a very muscular lean person as overfat (too heavy for height) or a lightweight person with little

muscular development and a large percentage of fat as being in the HFZ when the person is actually overfat.

In general, students who score in the Needs Improvement category should be encouraged to work toward the HFZ by slowly changing their body weight through increased physical activity and decreased consumption of high-calorie, low-nutrient foods. Changing dietary habits and exercise habits can be very difficult. Students with severe obesity or eating disorders may need professional assistance in their attempts to modify their behaviors. Evidence in adults clearly indicates that participation in regular physical activity moderates the health risks associated with obesity. Because this relationship likely holds true for children as well, emphasis for overweight children should be on being physically active and not on absolute weight or fat loss.

It is important to remember when interpreting body composition results that most students who are overfat may also have performances in other test areas that are outside the HFZ. An improvement in body composition will generally result in an improved performance in aerobic capacity and also muscular strength and endurance, especially in the upper body, due to a reduction in excess weight.

FITNESSGRAM also identifies students who are exceptionally lean. Students in this range (designated as very lean) receive a message indicating that being this lean may not be best for health. A score in the Very Lean category is treated as being in the HFZ with respect to the output on the *FITNESSGRAM* report.

Parents and teachers should notice students who are categorized as very lean and should consider factors that may be responsible for their low level of body fat. Many students may naturally be very lean, whereas others may have inappropriate nutritional patterns. A few students may have eating disorders. A factor to consider is whether the student's level of fat has suddenly changed from within the optimal range to a level identified as very lean. Severe changes may signal a potential problem. Creating awareness of a child's current status is the primary purpose in identifying lean students. Changes in status should be monitored.

FITNESSGRAM results can be very helpful in allowing students to follow changes in their levels of body fat over time. Obesity is a health problem for both children and adults, and results of tracking studies reveal that overweight and obesity track through the life span. To reduce problems with weight later in life, it is important to address the problem earlier, before the lifestyle patterns and physiological changes are firmly established.

Muscular Strength, Endurance, and Flexibility

Students who score poorly in one or more areas of muscle strength, endurance, and flexibility should be encouraged to participate in calisthenics and other strengthening and stretching activities that will develop those areas. However, it is essential to remember that physical fitness training is very specific and that the areas of the body being tested represent only a fraction of the total body.

To focus on activities that develop the extensors of the arms without equal attention to the flexors of the arms will not accomplish the important objective, which is to develop an overall healthy musculoskeletal system. Remember, you must have strength and flexibility in the muscles on both sides of every joint. A useful activity for all students is to identify exercises to strengthen and stretch the muscles at every major joint of the trunk, upper body, and lower body.

Poor performance on the measures of abdominal strength and trunk extensor strength and flexibility may merit special attention. Gaining strength and flexibility in these areas may help prevent low back pain, which affects millions of people, young and old.

Summary of Fitness Testing Principles

In interpreting performance on physical fitness assessments, it is most important to remember the following:

- The physical fitness experience should always be fun and enjoyable.
- Physical fitness testing should not become a competitive sport.
- The performance of one student should not be compared to that of another student.
- The primary reason for testing is to provide the student with personal information that may be used in planning a personal fitness program.
- The performance level on fitness tests should not be used as a basis for grading.

FITNESSGRAM does not advocate a recognition program that focuses primarily on fitness performance. Recognition should reinforce the establishment of physical activity behaviors that will lead to fitness development.

To further enhance communication with parents, the software offers a report written specifically for parents. Though the *FITNESSGRAM* student report provides some background information for parents, it primarily includes information for the student. The new *FITNESSGRAM* parent report includes information to help parents understand the assessment, the meaning of the results, and steps to take to help their child improve.

The *FITNESSGRAM* parent report includes

- a brief explanation of each assessment,
- details on the importance of each assessment,
- the child's actual scores and the Healthy Fitness Zone (HFZ) for the child's gender and age,
- an explanation of the HFZ and the student report,
- the philosophy that guides the FITNESSGRAM program,
- detailed information on their child's physical activity needs, and
- ideas for parents to help their child become more physically active.

This report will give parents a better understanding of the fitness assessment process, which may help them to assist their children in being physically active. It is very important that parents play a supportive role in their children's physical activity and fitness program.

PART III

ACTIVITYGRAM ASSESSMENT MODULE

ACTIVITYGRAM is a behaviorally based activity assessment tool that can help young children and adolescents learn more about their physical activity habits. The assessment is a three-day recall of the various activities performed. The predominant activity in each 30-minute block of time is coded, and the resulting data are used to determine the amount of time spent in activity, the times when a child is active or inactive, and the types of activity performed. Recommendations are based on national guidelines developed by the Council for Physical Education for Children (COPEC), a division of the National Association for Sport and Physical Education (NASPE).

Chapter 10 covers general principles associated with collecting accurate self-reported information on physical activity. Chapter 11 provides information on interpreting *ACTIVITYGRAM* test results.

ACTIVITYGRAM ADMINISTRATION

Because a major goal of physical education programs is promoting regular physical activity, it is important to include assessments of physical activity in the curriculum. While fitness is important, it cannot be maintained unless children are physically active. The *ACTIVITYGRAM* Physical Activity Recall provides a tool to assist teachers in offering instruction and feedback related to physical activity topics. To complete the assessment, children will need to be able to categorize different types of activity, describe the intensity of the activity, and estimate the length of time (duration) spent being physically active. The report provides detailed information about the child's activity habits and prescriptive feedback about how active he or she should be.

The *ACTIVITYGRAM* module was designed to be conducted as an "event" similar in focus and structure to the *FITNESSGRAM* assessments. Instructors are encouraged to provide time in the curriculum to teach concepts related to physical activity and to utilize this new evaluation tool. Because of the cognitive demands of recalling physical activity, it may be difficult for young children to get accurate results. For this reason, the *ACTIVITYGRAM* module is recommended for children in grades 5 and higher. However, if used for educational purposes only and if some training or assistance is provided, it still should be possible for younger children (grades 3 and 4) to obtain meaningful results. In order to use *ACTIVITYGRAM* in version 8.x, you must have the student application installed and allow the students to enter their own information (a sample image of the screen is shown later). This chapter describes the *ACTIVITYGRAM* module in more detail and provides guidelines for administering the instrument within physical education classes. Additional detail on the reliability and validity of different physical activity assessments is included in the *FITNESSGRAM Reference Guide* (see the chapter "Physical Activity Assessments" by Welk and Morrow).

Description of ACTIVITYGRAM

The *ACTIVITYGRAM* assessment is based conceptually on a validated physical activity instrument known as the Previous Day Physical Activity Recall

(PDPAR) (Weston, Petosa, and Pate, 1997). In the assessment the child is asked to report his or her activity levels for each 30-minute block of time during the day. The format is designed to accommodate both school and non-school days. Each assessment begins at 7:00 a.m. and continues until 11:00 p.m. For each 30-minute time block the child is asked to report the predominant activity for that interval. To help prompt the responses, the assessment provides children with a list of common activities. The activities are divided into categories based on the concept of the physical activity pyramid (Lifestyle Activity, Aerobic Activity, Aerobic Sports, Muscular Activity, Flexibility Activity, and Rest).

The pyramid provides a useful way to describe the variety of physical activities that contribute to good health. **Level 1** of the pyramid includes lifestyle activities, or activities that can be done as part of daily living. Activities at this level include walking to school, riding a bike, raking leaves, and general outdoor play of all kinds. **Level 2** of the pyramid includes a variety of aerobic sports and aerobic activities. Activities in **Level 3** include flexibility and muscle fitness activities. **Level 4** refers to rest activities such as homework, TV viewing, or eating. It is important for children to be able to categorize the activities they do so they can increase their involvement in healthy physical activity and minimize the amount of free time they spend in inactive pursuits such as TV viewing. See figure 10.1 for a conceptual model of the physical activity pyramid used in *ACTIVITYGRAM*.

For each activity that is selected on the assessment, students are prompted to indicate whether they were active in this activity for *"all of the time"* or just *"some of the time."* This effectively allows each interval to be represented as two 15-minute bouts rather than one 30-minute bout (i.e., if a student indicates that he or she was active *"all of the time,"* the student will be considered as having been active for two 15-minute bouts. If a student indicates that he or she was active *"some of the time,"* the student will be considered as having been active for one 15-minute bout). This distinction improves the accuracy of the assessment and also reinforces to the child that activity does not have to be continuous or done for long periods of time. If a child selects an activity from the Rest category, then the duration of the activity is assumed to be 30 minutes. A student cannot select *"some of the time"* for Rest because students who were resting for only a portion of the time should indicate what other type of activity they were performing in that time interval.

After selecting a duration, students are also asked to rate the intensity of the activity (Light, Moderate, Vigorous). The descriptors for the intensity levels were selected to be consistent with current physical activity guidelines that describe recommended levels of moderate and vigorous physical activity. See table 10.1 to distinguish among the different intensities.

Administration

The *ACTIVITYGRAM* module is accessed through the student application of the *FITNESSGRAM* software (see sample screen in figure 10.2). As previously mentioned, this module was designed to be administered as an "event" similar in scope to *FITNESSGRAM*. Teachers typically spend several weeks preparing for and completing the different fitness assessments, and this same level of attention should be devoted to administering the *ACTIVITYGRAM* assessment. If this module is established as an important part of the curriculum, children will put forth a better effort and there will be more cooperation with other teachers regarding scheduling time in computer labs and for completing the assessments. Involvement of parents to remind children to complete logs of their daily activities can also help improve the accuracy of the assessment and involvement of the students.

Obtaining accurate information about physical activity with self-report instruments is inherently challenging, and these challenges are magnified for assessments in children. The *ACTIVITYGRAM* software provides an intuitive computer interface and some built-in aids to facilitate the child's recall of physical activity. However, before the data collection is to take place, it is important to teach children about the different types and intensities of physical activity so they can more accurately distinguish the activities they do. A sample protocol is shown at the end of this chapter. This protocol provides only a rough outline of how the instrument can be introduced, and further refinement or customization may be needed. This type of instruction will enhance the educational value of the *ACTIVITYGRAM* assessment and improve the accuracy of the results.

Most teachers have students practice fitness assessments before testing, and this same guideline would apply to activity assessments as well. A sample logging page (Sample *ACTIVITYGRAM* Log) is provided in appendix B to facilitate this type of practice session during a portion of a physical education class. It is recommended that all students complete this practice log briefly before they complete the *ACTIVITYGRAM* for the first time. The

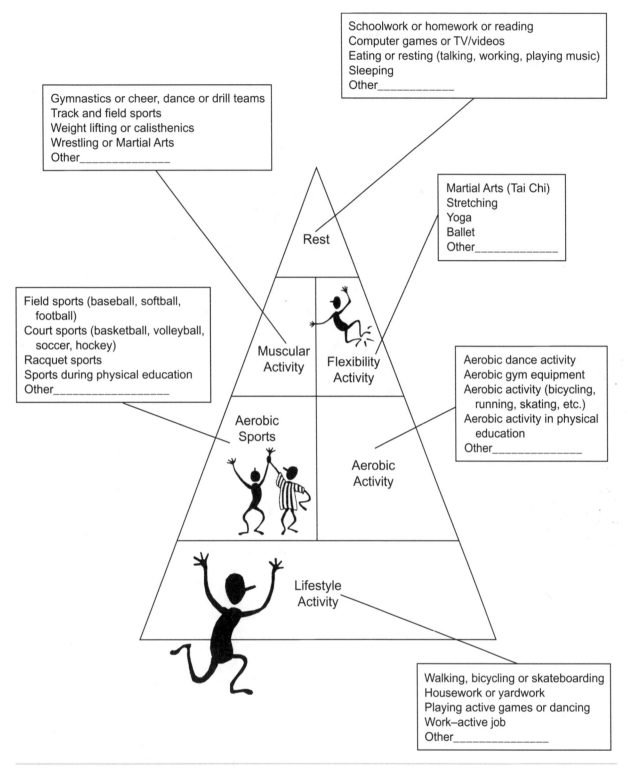

Schoolwork or homework or reading
Computer games or TV/videos
Eating or resting (talking, working, playing music)
Sleeping
Other_____

Gymnastics or cheer, dance or drill teams
Track and field sports
Weight lifting or calisthenics
Wrestling or Martial Arts
Other_____

Martial Arts (Tai Chi)
Stretching
Yoga
Ballet
Other_____

Rest

Field sports (baseball, softball,
    football)
Court sports (basketball, volleyball,
    soccer, hockey)
Racquet sports
Sports during physical education
Other_____

Muscular
Activity

Flexibility
Activity

Aerobic dance activity
Aerobic gym equipment
Aerobic activity (bicycling,
    running, skating, etc.)
Aerobic activity in physical
    education
Other_____

Aerobic
Sports

Aerobic
Activity

Lifestyle
Activity

Walking, bicycling or skateboarding
Housework or yardwork
Playing active games or dancing
Work–active job
Other_____

FIGURE 10.1 *ACTIVITYGRAM* pyramid.

TABLE 10.1	**Descriptions of Intensity Levels**
Light	Little or no movement, no increase in breathing rate, easy
Moderate	Movement equal in intensity to a brisk walk, some increase in breathing rate, not too difficult
Vigorous (hard)	Moving quickly, breathing hard, hard effort level

Note: Rest is defaulted to an intensity level of Very light.

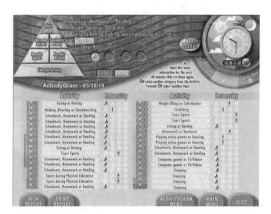

FIGURE 10.2   Sample *ACTIVITYGRAM* screen.

following protocol can be used to instruct students in how to complete the practice log.

> To practice learning about activity, I would like to have you try to remember what you did yesterday after school. Think back to yesterday and write down the main activity that you did for each 30-minute period after school. You can write the name of the activity in the space or use the chart at the bottom of the page to write down the number. For each activity, estimate the intensity as either REST, LIGHT, MODERATE, or VIGOROUS. *(Help the students select activities from the pyramid and rate the intensities.)*

While the instrument is intended to be a "recall" of the previous day's activity, accuracy may be improved by having children complete a detailed activity log during the day. This will help them more accurately recall what they actually did when they come into the computer lab. The use of a log may not be necessary if the children recall only one day back in time, but it is strongly recommended for extended days of recall. A copy master labeled "*ACTIVITY-GRAM* Assessment" is provided in appendix B (page 107). This page can be photocopied and put into a booklet for all students as part of the *ACTIVITYGRAM* assessment. Providing information to parents on a cover page would help to promote parental involvement and support and provide a reminder to the children. Requiring the completion of the log as a "participation activity" (i.e., as homework) is another way to promote compliance with the monitoring protocol.

A sample *ACTIVITYGRAM* Instruction Booklet is included on the Test Administration DVD.

If the child completes at least two days of assessments, the results are printed as the *ACTIVITYGRAM* report. The report includes information regarding the amount of activity performed, activity patterns throughout the day, and the type of activities performed as classified by the Activity Pyramid. Consult the next chapter, "Interpreting *ACTIVITYGRAM* Results," to find out how the results are compiled and summarized.

Sample Training Protocol
for Instruction on *ACTIVITYGRAM*

Orientation to *ACTIVITYGRAM*

Over the next few days you are going to learn about the types and amounts of physical activity that you do in a normal day. While you get some activity in physical education, you probably do a lot of other activities after school or at home. The assessment that we will do will allow you to track the different activities you do over three different days. You will need to record the main activity you do for each 30-minute block of time in the day. While you may do a lot of different activities, you will need to record only the main activity that you did during that time. The activities will be selected using the Activity Pyramid *(describe the Activity Pyramid using the copy master in the manual or with a wall chart).* For each activity, you will then rate the intensity of the activity as either **REST, LIGHT, MODERATE,** or **VIGOROUS** and then specify how long you did it.

Explanation About Physical Activity

Physical activity refers to movements that require the use of your large muscles (such as your arms and legs) and that make you breathe hard or sweat. **Can anyone give me some examples of physical activity?** There are also a lot of different resting activities that you might do during the day. **Can anyone give me some examples of some things they like to do when they are resting or relaxing?** The Activity Pyramid provides a way to categorize the different types of activities that you do. In the *ACTIVITYGRAM* assessment you will use this pyramid to help you pick the different activities that you do. *(Summarize the different parts of the pyramid in more detail.)*

- **Lifestyle activities** are things you do as part of your normal day (walking, bike riding, playing, housework, or yard work).
- **Aerobic activities** are things you do to improve your aerobic fitness (e.g., jogging, bike riding, swimming, dancing).
- **Aerobic sports** are sports that involve a lot of movement. These may be sports you do for fun with a few people or ones that you do as part of a team.
- **Muscular activities** are things that require a lot of strength.
- **Flexibility activities** are things that might involve stretching your muscles.

   Can you think of some things that you do that are not on the list? If you do an activity that is not listed, you should pick the category that it belongs in and choose the "Other" activity provided in each category. For example, if you were riding in a car, what type of activity would that be? (answer = OTHER REST). If you were climbing trees, what might you

(continued)

(continued)

select? (OTHER MUSCULAR). If you were just playing around the house, the activity might involve a lot of different movements, but you would probably just select OTHER LIFESTYLE. It is important to remember that most activities that you do are probably LIGHT or REST. You might only have a few periods each day when you might be running or playing a bit harder.

Explanation About Intensity

Activities can be done at different intensities. An activity that mostly involves sitting or standing but little motion can be considered a **REST** activity (example = sitting in class or reading). An activity that involves slow movements but is not too tiring might be called **LIGHT** (example = slow walk or stroll).

An activity that involves quick movements or running, or one that makes you breathe hard, would be called **VIGOROUS** (example = fast jog). Activities that are between LIGHT and VIGOROUS would be called **MODERATE** (brisk walk). *Provide students with examples of different activities and have them rate the intensity. Remind them again about the types of things that would count as REST (sitting in a car, listening to music, talking with friends, and so on).*

Explanation About Duration

Activity can be done for various periods of time. You might be active for a few minutes and then rest for a few minutes. This is a good way to stay active throughout the day. In the activity assessment you complete, you will pick the main activity you do in each 30-minute period. If you did this for only a part of the time, you will have the option of selecting **SOME OF THE TIME** for the duration of the activity.

CHAPTER 11

INTERPRETING ACTIVITYGRAM RESULTS

The *ACTIVITYGRAM* Physical Activity Recall provides detailed information about a child's normal physical activity patterns. If children complete at least two days of assessments, the results can be summarized and printed on the *ACTIVITYGRAM* report. The report includes information regarding the amount of activity performed, activity patterns throughout the day, and the type of activities performed. See figure 11.1 for a sample *ACTIVITYGRAM* report.

The criterion-referenced standards used to determine feedback on the *ACTIVITYGRAM* reports are based on youth physical activity guidelines published by the Council for Physical Activity for Children (COPEC) and the National Association of Sports and Physical Education (NASPE). These guidelines specify that children should perform a variety of activities and that the typical intermittent activity patterns of children should be encouraged. The guidelines are summarized on page 83.

Providing Feedback to Children on ACTIVITYGRAM

It is important to help children learn how to interpret their *ACTIVITYGRAM* report, so you should devote time during class to going over the different components of the report. The following sections provide information that may help to explain the results for each category of the report.

Need Additional Information?

For additional information on physical activity assessment and the reliability of the *ACTIVITYGRAM* assessment, see the *FITNESSGRAM Reference Guide*. The *Guide* is available on the enclosed DVD or online at the *FITNESSGRAM* Web site, www.fitnessgram.net (go to the *Reference Guide* section). Read the chapter titled "Physical Activity Assessments" by Welk and Morrow.

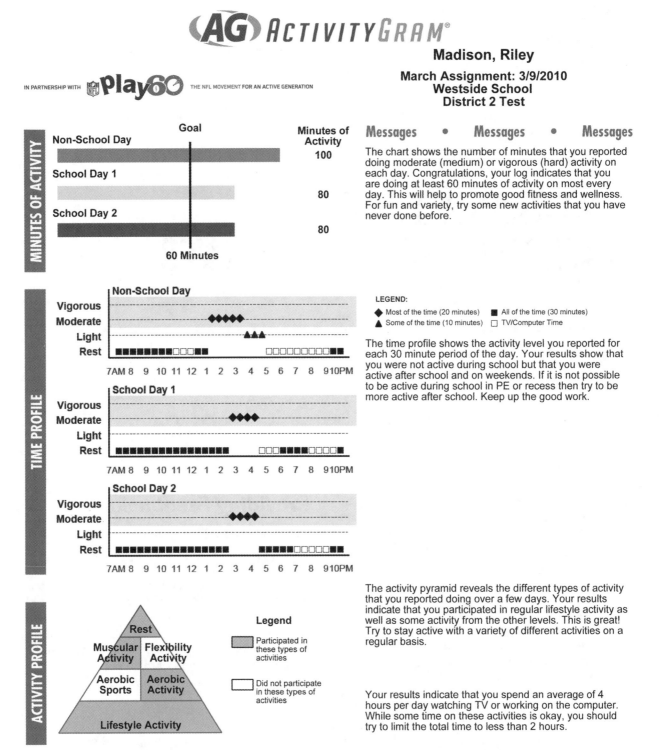

FIGURE 11.1 Sample *ACTIVITYGRAM* computer report.

> # Guidelines for Children's Physical Activity
>
> - Elementary school-aged children should accumulate at least 30 to 60 minutes of age-appropriate and developmentally appropriate physical activity on most days of the week.
>
> - An accumulation of more than 60 minutes is encouraged for children.
>
> - Some of the child's activity each day should include moderate to vigorous activity in periods lasting 10 to 15 minutes.
>
> - Extended periods of inactivity are inappropriate for children.
>
> - A variety of activities from the Physical Activity Pyramid are recommended for children.

Minutes of Physical Activity

The approach taken in the *ACTIVITYGRAM* report is to focus on the attainment of regular, moderately intense physical activity. The Healthy Activity Zone is set at 60 minutes of activity each day. This value is higher than the typical recommendation for adults of 30 minutes per day since it is important for children to establish regular patterns of activity early in life. There is a general tendency for children to overestimate activity levels using the *ACTIVITYGRAM* assessments so the higher standard also protects against this possible bias. Teachers should be aware that bouts of activity that are not at the moderate or vigorous level are **not** included in the total number of minutes. No distinction is made between moderate and vigorous activity in this assessment. This reinforces to children that physical activity is for everyone and that activity doesn't have to be vigorous to be beneficial.

Time Profile

The time profile indicates the times when students report having been physically active. Bouts of moderate and vigorous activity would correspond to levels 3 and 4 on the graphical report. Emphasis in the interpretation of the time profile should be placed on helping students identify times when they could be more active. Because school time is often out of a student's control, the feedback for this section highlights activity patterns after school and on weekends. For a child to be considered "active" on this section of the report, he or she must have at least 30 minutes of moderate or vigorous activity before or after school and at least 60 minutes of moderate or vigorous activity on the weekend day. Feedback can be provided individually or to the class to help them identify times when they could be more active.

Activity Profile

The activity profile categorizes the types of activities performed by the child based on the conceptual categories included in the physical activity pyramid described by Corbin and Pangrazi (1998). Ideally, children would have some activity at each level of the pyramid. Lifestyle activity is recommended for all students (and adults). If students are not performing much activity, the recommendation is to first try promoting lifestyle activity. From a health perspective, aerobic activity on the second level can correct for a lack of lifestyle activity on the first level, but it is still desirable to promote lifestyle activity among all students. No distinctions are needed between the two types of aerobic activity on the second level. Some children may prefer aerobic activities whereas others may prefer aerobic sports. Participation in either of those categories would ensure that the student is engaging in reasonable amounts of aerobic activity. Some distinction can be made at the level of musculoskeletal activity (level 3). Students should perform some activity from both the strength and flexibility categories, but there is likely to be some transfer between activities from the two categories. Rest is coded at the top of the pyramid because levels of inactivity should be minimized. The feedback regarding this level does not mention nondiscretionary activities like class, homework, eating, or sleeping. Rather, emphasis is placed on making children (and parents) aware of the child's use of discretionary time. For this reason, feedback is provided for the amount of time spent playing computer games or watching television. Lifestyle activities are not evaluated based on intensity. The bout of activity is counted if a lifestyle activity was performed for 20 minutes.

Limitations of the ACTIVITYGRAM Assessment

When interpreting the results of the *ACTIVI-TYGRAM*, it is important to acknowledge the limitations of this assessment. Obtaining accurate information on physical activity from self-report measures is difficult for all populations but is even more challenging among youth. In addition to problems with recall, there are other difficulties that complicate this type of assessment. Children have inherently sporadic activity patterns that are difficult to capture with a self-report instrument. The instrument provides a limited list of possible activities and relies on categorization of activity into discrete time intervals. This may not reflect the normal patterns of children. An additional limitation is that the results of this assessment may not generalize to the child's normal activity pattern. *ACTIVITYGRAM* reflects only 2 to 3 days of activity, and experts agree that about 7 days of monitoring is required to accurately represent normal activity habits. While these limitations may influence the accuracy of the test, they do not detract from the educational value it contributes in the curriculum.

The recommendation here is to acknowledge the limitations of the instrument and use it for its primary function: teaching children about physical activity. Even if results are not completely accurate, the task of reflecting on their activity habits will provide children with a valuable educational experience.

INFORMATION ON TESTING EQUIPMENT

Sources of Testing Equipment

The PACER Music CDs
Human Kinetics
P.O. Box 5076
Champaign, IL 61825-5076
800-747-4457

Skinfold Calipers
Human Kinetics
P.O. Box 5076
Champaign, IL 61825-5076
800-747-4457

Training Films on Skinfold Measurement
Human Kinetics
P.O. Box 5076
Champaign, IL 61825-5076
800-747-4457

Curl-Up Measuring Strips
Human Kinetics
P.O. Box 5076
Champaign, IL 61825-5076
800-747-4457

Measuring Strip for Curl-Up Test

Cut from poster board (see figure A.1).

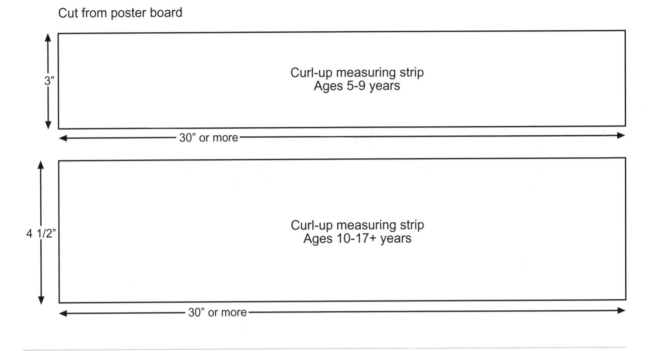

FIGURE A.1

Other Suggestions for Measuring Curl-Up Distances

There are any number of methods to measure the distance attained in the curl-up test. The important factor is to ensure that the student is moving the fingertips 3 inches for ages 5 to 9 years and 4 1/2 inches for ages 10 and above. Another factor to consider is that the student should be able to "feel" the stopping point rather than rely on "seeing" it. Do not be afraid to experiment with other methods to measure this distance. The following suggestions are alternative methods that could be used.

1. Use tape and a pencil to indicate the marks. Put tape on the mat at the starting point for the fingertips. Tape a pencil to the mat parallel to the starting line at the stopping point (3 inches or 4 1/2 inches).

2. Permanent measuring strips like those shown in figure A.1 could be cut from a sheet of 1/4-inch plywood. These would need to be carefully sanded to prevent splinters. Laminated poster board would also provide more permanent measuring strips.

3. Measuring cards could be cut to the appropriate width (3 or 4 1/2 inches) out of index cards. Two would be needed for every two students. Cards would need to be taped to the mat in position for the student to slide the fingers from one edge of the card to the other.

Equipment for Modified Pull-Up

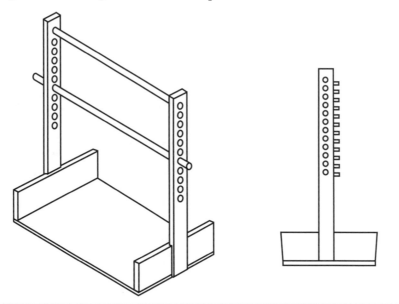

FIGURE A.2

Items needed:

Two 2 × 4 × 48-inch pieces for uprights.

Two 2 × 8 × 24-inch pieces for base of uprights.

One piece of 3/4-inch plywood, 24 × 39 inches, for support platform

One 1 1/8-inch steel pipe for chinning bar, at least 43 inches long

One 1 1/4-inch dowel for top support, 39 inches long

Twenty-four 3/8-inch dowel pieces cut 3 1/2 inches long

Nails, wood screws, and wood glue for construction

1. Beginning 2 1/2 inches from the top end of each 2 × 4 × 48 piece, drill one hole through the 2-inch thickness for the 1 1/4-inch dowel support rod.

2. In each piece, drill 11 more 1 1/8-inch holes below the first hole, spaced 2 1/2 inches from center to center, for the steel pipe.

3. Beginning 3 3/4 inches from the top of these upright pieces, drill twelve 3/8-inch holes into the 4-inch thickness for the dowel pieces. Center these holes between the holes for the steel pipe.

4. Assemble the pieces and finish with polyurethane or shellac.

Equipment for Back-Saver Sit and Reach

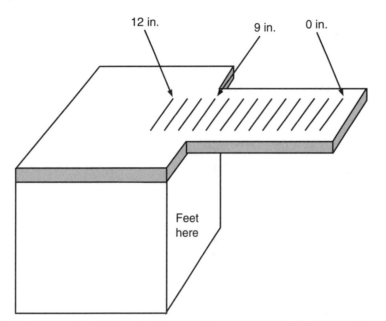

FIGURE A.3

Items needed:

1. Using any sturdy wood or comparable material (3/4-inch plywood seems to work well), cut the following pieces:

Two pieces 12 × 12 inches

Two pieces 12 × 10 1/2 inches

One piece 12 × 22 inches

2. Cut 10 × 4-inch pieces from each side of one end of the 12 × 22-inch piece to make the top of the box. Beginning at the small end, mark 1-inch intervals up to 12 inches.

3. Construct a box (use nails, screws, or wood glue) with the remaining four pieces. Attach the top. It is crucial that the 9-inch mark be exactly parallel with the vertical plane against which the subject's foot will be placed. The 0-inch mark is at the end nearest the subject.

4. Cover the apparatus with polyurethane sealer or shellac.

Alternative Flexibility Testing Apparatus

1. Use a sturdy cardboard box at least 12 inches tall. Turn the box so that the bottom is up. Tape a yardstick to the bottom. The yardstick must be placed so that the 9-inch mark is exactly parallel with the vertical plane against which the subject's foot will be placed and the 0-inch end is nearer the subject.

2. Use a bench that is about 12 inches wide. Turn the bench on its side. Tape a yardstick to the bench so that the 9-inch mark is exactly parallel with the vertical plane against which the subject's foot will be placed and the 0-inch end is nearer the subject.

COPY MASTERS

Contents

Student name _____

Get Fit Conditioning Program

The GetFit Conditioning Program is a six-week program designed to help you get in shape for your fitness test.
   Guidelines are as follows:

   Participate at least three times each week for six weeks.

   Complete the exercise log and return it to your teacher.

   You may do some of your workouts during your physical education class.

   Select activities from this appendix or do your favorite activities from physical education class.

   Place a check mark in the box for each day you work out. Your workout should include a warm-up, strength development, aerobic activities, and a cool-down.

Warm-up: At the beginning of the workout do at least three warm-up exercises. Move easily at first and gradually get faster. Hold a stretch for 10 counts and do not bounce. Be sure to do work for the upper body and the legs.

Strength development: Do at least three strength exercises. Do as many of each exercise as you can up to 20.

Aerobic activity: Begin with 2 to 5 minutes of your activity and gradually increase the time to 25 to 30 minutes.

Cool-down: Do three of your favorite activities from figure B.2. Be sure to stretch upper and lower body and trunk.

	Sunday	Monday	Tuesday	Wednesday	Thursday	Friday	Saturday
Week 1 Date:							
Week 2 Date:							
Week 3 Date:							
Week 4 Date:							
Week 5 Date:							
Week 6 Date:							
Week 7 Date:							

FIGURE B.1

From *FITNESSGRAM/ACTIVITYGRAM Test Administration Manual, Updated Fourth Edition* by The Cooper Institute, 2010, Champaign, IL: Human Kinetics.

FITNESSGRAM Get Fit Exercises

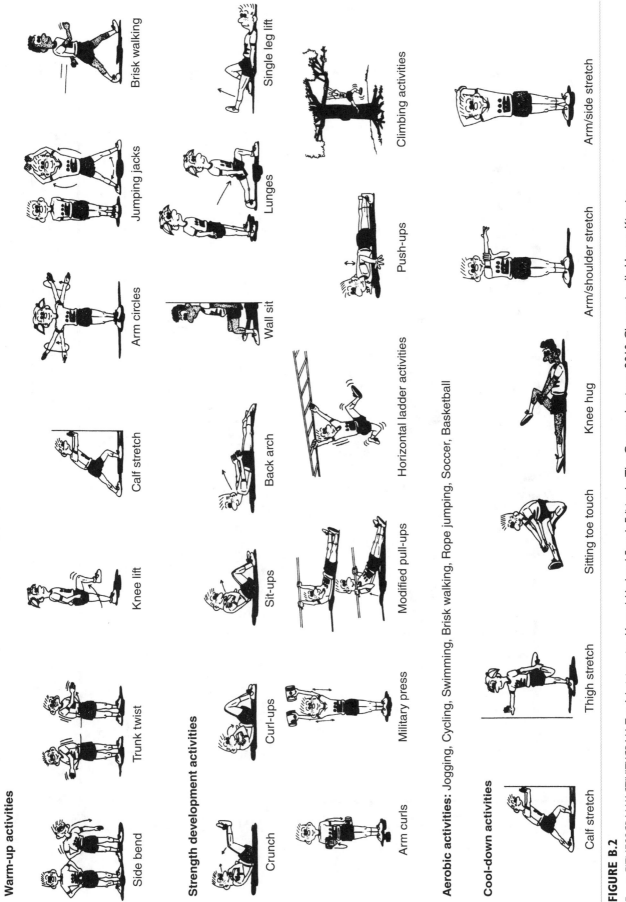

Warm-up activities

Side bend | Trunk twist | Knee lift | Calf stretch | Arm circles | Jumping jacks | Brisk walking

Strength development activities

Crunch | Curl-ups | Sit-ups | Back arch | Wall sit | Single leg lift

Arm curls | Military press | Modified pull-ups | Horizontal ladder activities | Push-ups | Lunges | Climbing activities

Aerobic activities: Jogging, Cycling, Swimming, Brisk walking, Rope jumping, Soccer, Basketball

Cool-down activities

Calf stretch | Thigh stretch | Sitting toe touch | Knee hug | Arm/shoulder stretch | Arm/side stretch

FIGURE B.2

From *FITNESSGRAM/ACTIVITYGRAM Test Administration Manual, Updated Fourth Edition* by The Cooper Institute, 2010, Champaign, IL: Human Kinetics.

FITNESSGRAM/ACTIVITYGRAM

Get Fit Award

This certifies that

____

has successfully completed the "Get Fit" activity program and demonstrated outstanding commitment to developing good fitness habits.

Date ______________ ______________

FIGURE B.3

From *FITNESSGRAM/ACTIVITYGRAM Test Administration Manual, Updated Fourth Edition* by The Cooper Institute, 2010, Champaign, IL: Human Kinetics.

FITNESSGRAM

Physical Activity Goals

Week of _____

My plans are to do

	Activity I plan to do	Time of day	Friend(s) who will be active with me
Monday			
Tuesday			
Wednesday			
Thursday			
Friday			
Saturday			
Sunday			

Date _____ Student's signature _____ Teacher's initials _____

The actual activity I did

	Yes, I did the following activity	How long?	I was unable to do planned activity because
Monday			
Tuesday			
Wednesday			
Thursday			
Friday			
Saturday			
Sunday			

FIGURE B.4

From *FITNESSGRAM/ACTIVITYGRAM Test Administration Manual, Updated Fourth Edition* by The Cooper Institute, 2010, Champaign, IL: Human Kinetics.

FITNESS CONTRACT

I, _____, agree to:

When I complete the requirements listed above,
I will receive appropriate recognition of my activity.

Student's Signature _____

Date _____

I agree that the student named above will be
recognized for completing the terms of
this contract by receiving

_____

Teacher's Signature _____

Date _____

FIGURE B.5

From *FITNESSGRAM/ACTIVITYGRAM Test Administration Manual, Updated Fourth Edition* by The Cooper Institute, 2010, Champaign, IL: Human Kinetics.

FITNESSGRAM

The PACER Individual Score Sheet A

Teacher _____   Class period _____   Date _____

Lap = one 20-meter length

Level	Laps												
1	1	2	3	4	5	6	7						
2	8	9	10	11	12	13	14	15					
3	16	17	18	19	20	21	22	23					
4	24	25	26	27	28	29	30	31	32				
5	33	34	35	36	37	38	39	40	41				
6	42	43	44	45	46	47	48	49	50	51			
7	52	53	54	55	56	57	58	59	60	61			
8	62	63	64	65	66	67	68	69	70	71	72		
9	73	74	75	76	77	78	79	80	81	82	83		
10	84	85	86	87	88	89	90	91	92	93	94		
11	95	96	97	98	99	100	101	102	103	104	105	106	
12	107	108	109	110	111	112	113	114	115	116	117	118	
13	119	120	121	122	123	124	125	126	127	128	129	130	131
14	132	133	134	135	136	137	138	139	140	141	142	143	144
15	145	146	147	148	149	150	151	152	153	154	155	156	157

Lane _____   Student's signature _____   Laps completed _____

FIGURE B.6

From *FITNESSGRAM/ACTIVITYGRAM Test Administration Manual, Updated Fourth Edition* by The Cooper Institute, 2010, Champaign, IL: Human Kinetics.

FITNESSGRAM PACER Test Individual Score Sheet B

Student Name _____   Class _____   Date _____

FIGURE B.7

From *FITNESSGRAM/ACTIVITYGRAM Test Administration Manual, Updated Fourth Edition* by The Cooper Institute, 2010, Champaign, IL: Human Kinetics.

FITNESSGRAM

The PACER Group Score Sheet

Teacher _____ Class period _____ Date _____

Lap = one 20-meter length

Level	Laps												
1	1	2	3	4	5	6	7						
2	8	9	10	11	12	13	14	15					
3	16	17	18	19	20	21	22	23					
4	24	25	26	27	28	29	30	31	32				
5	33	34	35	36	37	38	39	40	41				
6	42	43	44	45	46	47	48	49	50	51			
7	52	53	54	55	56	57	58	59	60	61			
8	62	63	64	65	66	67	68	69	70	71	72		
9	73	74	75	76	77	78	79	80	81	82	83		
10	84	85	86	87	88	89	90	91	92	93	94		
11	95	96	97	98	99	100	101	102	103	104	105	106	
12	107	108	109	110	111	112	113	114	115	116	117	118	
13	119	120	121	122	123	124	125	126	127	128	129	130	131
14	132	133	134	135	136	137	138	139	140	141	142	143	144
15	145	146	147	148	149	150	151	152	153	154	155	156	157

Lane	Student name	Laps completed	Lane	Student name	Laps completed

FIGURE B.8

From *FITNESSGRAM/ACTIVITYGRAM Test Administration Manual, Updated Fourth Edition* by The Cooper Institute, 2010, Champaign, IL: Human Kinetics.

PACER Conversion Chart

Use this chart to convert scores on the 15–M PACER to a 20–M score to enter in the *FITNESSGRAM* software.

Level		Laps 1	2	3	4	5	6	7	8	9	10	11	12	13	14	15	16	17	18	19	20
1	15 M	1																			
	20 M	1																			
2	15 M	10	11	12	13	14	15	16	17	18	19										
	20 M	8	8	9	10	11	12	12	13	14	15										
3	15 M	20	21	22	23	24	25	26	27	28	29	30									
	20 M	15	16	17	18	18	19	20	21	22	22	23									
4	15 M	31	32	33	34	35	36	37	38	39	40	41	42								
	20 M	24	25	25	26	27	28	28	29	30	31	32	32								
5	15 M	43	44	45	46	47	48	49	50	51	52	53	54								
	20 M	33	34	35	35	36	37	38	38	39	40	41	41								
6	15 M	55	56	57	58	59	60	61	62	63	64	65	66	67							
	20 M	42	43	44	45	45	46	47	48	48	49	50	51	51							
7	15 M	68	69	70	71	72	73	74	75	76	77	78	79	80							
	20 M	52	53	54	55	55	56	57	58	58	59	60	61	61							
8	15 M	81	82	83	84	85	86	87	88	89	90	91	92	93	94						
	20 M	62	63	64	65	65	66	67	68	68	69	70	71	72	72						
9	15 M	95	96	97	98	99	100	101	102	103	104	105	106	107	108						
	20 M	73	74	75	75	76	77	78	78	79	80	81	82	82	83						
10	15 M	109	110	111	112	113	114	115	116	117	118	119	120	121	122	123					
	20 M	84	85	85	86	87	88	88	89	90	91	92	92	93	94	94					
11	15 M	124	125	126	127	128	129	130	131	132	133	134	135	136	137	138					
	20 M	95	96	97	98	98	99	100	101	102	102	103	104	105	105	106					
12	15 M	139	140	141	142	143	144	145	146	147	148	149	150	151	152	153	154				
	20 M	107	108	108	109	110	111	111	112	113	114	114	115	116	117	117	118				
13	15 M	155	156	157	158	159	160	161	162	163	164	165	166	167	168	169	170	171			
	20 M	119	120	121	121	122	123	124	124	125	126	127	128	128	129	130	130	131			
14	15 M	172	173	174	175	176	177	178	179	180	181	182	183	184	185	186	187	188			
	20 M	132	133	134	134	135	136	137	137	138	139	140	140	141	142	143	143	144			
15	15 M	189	190	191	192	193	194	195	196	197	198	199	200	201	202	203	204	205	206		
	20 M	145	146	147	147	148	149	149	150	151	152	152	153	154	154	155	156	156	157		
16	15 M	207	208	209	210	211	212	213	214	215	216	217	218	219	220	221	222	223	224		
	20 M	158	159	160	160	161	162	163	163	164	165	166	166	167	168	169	169	170	171		
17	15 M	225	226	227	228	229	230	231	232	233	234	235	236	237	238	239	240	241	242	243	
	20 M	172	173	174	174	175	176	177	177	178	179	179	180	181	181	182	183	184	184	185	
18	15 M	244	245	246	247	248	249	250	251	252	253	254	255	256	257	258	259	260	261	262	
	20 M	186	187	188	188	189	190	190	191	192	193	193	194	195	196	197	197	198	199	200	
19	15 M	263	264	265	266	267	268	269	270	271	272	273	274	275	276	277	278	279	280	281	282
	20 M	201	202	203	203	204	205	206	206	207	208	208	209	210	210	211	212	213	214	214	
20	15 M	283	284	285	286	287	288	289	290	291	292	293	294	295	296	297	298	299	300	301	
	20 M	216	217	218	218	219	220	221	221	222	223	224	224	225	226	227	228	229	230	230	

One-Mile Run Individual Score Sheet

Runner Name: _____

Scorer Name: _____

Laps Completed (cross off each lap number as your runner completes it)

1   2   3   4   5   6   7   8   9   10

11   12   13   14   15   16   17   18   19   20

Finish Time: _____

✂ -

One-Mile Run Individual Score Sheet

Runner Name: _____

Scorer Name: _____

Laps Completed (cross off each lap number as your runner completes it)

1   2   3   4   5   6   7   8   9   10

11   12   13   14   15   16   17   18   19   20

Finish Time: _____

FIGURE B.9

From *FITNESSGRAM/ACTIVITYGRAM Test Administration Manual, Updated Fourth Edition* by The Cooper Institute, 2010, Champaign, IL: Human Kinetics.

Walk Test Individual Score Sheet

Runner Name: _____

Scorer Name: _____

Laps Completed (cross off each lap number as your runner completes it)

1	2	3	4	5	6	7	8	9	10
11	12	13	14	15	16	17	18	19	20

Finish Time: _____

Heart Rate: _____

✂- -

Walk Test Individual Score Sheet

Runner Name: _____

Scorer Name: _____

Laps Completed (cross off each lap number as your runner completes it)

1	2	3	4	5	6	7	8	9	10
11	12	13	14	15	16	17	18	19	20

Finish Time: _____

Heart Rate: _____

FIGURE B.10

From *FITNESSGRAM/ACTIVITYGRAM Test Administration Manual, Updated Fourth Edition* by The Cooper Institute, 2010, Champaign, IL: Human Kinetics.

FITNESSGRAM Body Composition Conversion Chart

						BOYS				
Total MM	**% Fat**	**Total MM**	**% Fat**	**Total MM**	**% Fat**	**Total MM**	**% Fat**	**Total MM**	**% Fat**
1.0	1.7	16.0	12.8	31.0	23.8	46.0	34.8	61.0	45.8
1.5	2.1	16.5	13.1	31.5	24.2	46.5	35.2	61.5	46.2
2.0	2.5	17.0	13.5	32.0	24.5	47.0	35.5	62.0	46.6
2.5	2.8	17.5	13.9	32.5	24.9	47.5	35.9	62.5	46.9
3.0	3.2	18.0	14.2	33.0	25.3	48.0	36.3	63.0	47.3
3.5	3.6	18.5	14.6	33.5	25.6	48.5	36.6	63.5	47.7
4.0	3.9	19.0	15.0	34.0	26.0	49.0	37.0	64.0	48.0
4.5	4.3	19.5	15.3	34.5	26.4	49.5	37.4	64.5	48.4
5.0	4.7	20.0	15.7	35.0	26.7	50.0	37.8	65.0	48.8
5.5	5.0	20.5	16.1	35.5	27.1	50.5	38.1	65.5	49.1
6.0	5.4	21.0	16.4	36.0	27.5	51.0	38.5	66.0	49.5
6.5	5.8	21.5	16.8	36.5	27.8	51.5	38.9	66.5	49.9
7.0	6.1	22.0	17.2	37.0	28.2	52.0	39.2	67.0	50.2
7.5	6.5	22.5	17.5	37.5	28.6	52.5	39.6	67.5	50.6
8.0	6.9	23.0	17.9	38.0	28.9	53.0	40.0	68.0	51.0
8.5	7.2	23.5	18.3	38.5	29.3	53.5	40.3	68.5	51.3
9.0	7.6	24.0	18.6	39.0	29.7	54.0	40.7	69.0	51.7
9.5	8.0	24.5	19.0	39.5	30.0	54.5	41.1	69.5	52.1
10.0	8.4	25.0	19.4	40.0	30.4	55.0	41.4	70.0	52.5
10.5	8.7	25.5	19.7	40.5	30.8	55.5	41.8	70.5	52.8
11.0	9.1	26.0	20.1	41.0	31.1	56.0	42.2	71.0	53.2
11.5	9.5	26.5	20.5	41.5	31.5	56.5	42.5	71.5	53.6
12.0	9.8	27.0	20.8	42.0	31.9	57.0	42.9	72.0	53.9
12.5	10.2	27.5	21.2	42.5	32.2	57.5	43.3	72.5	54.3
13.0	10.6	28.0	21.6	43.0	32.6	58.0	43.6	73.0	54.7
13.5	10.9	28.5	21.9	43.5	33.0	58.5	44.0	73.5	55.0
14.0	11.3	29.0	22.3	44.0	33.3	59.0	44.4	74.0	55.4
14.5	11.7	29.5	22.7	44.5	33.7	59.5	44.7	74.5	55.8
15.0	12.0	30.0	23.1	45.0	34.1	60.0	45.1	75.0	56.1
15.5	12.4	30.5	23.4	45.5	34.4	60.5	45.5	75.5	56.5

From *FITNESSGRAM/ACTIVITYGRAM Test Administration Manual, Updated Fourth Edition* by The Cooper Institute, 2010, Champaign, IL: Human Kinetics.

TABLE B.2 **_FITNESSGRAM_ Body Composition Conversion Chart**

GIRLS									
Total MM	**% Fat**	**Total MM**	**% Fat**	**Total MM**	**% Fat**	**Total MM**	**% Fat**	**Total MM**	**% Fat**
1.0	5.7	16.0	14.9	31.0	24.0	46.0	33.2	61.0	42.3
1.5	6.0	16.5	15.2	31.5	24.3	46.5	33.5	61.5	42.6
2.0	6.3	17.0	15.5	32.0	24.6	47.0	33.8	62.0	42.9
2.5	6.6	17.5	15.8	32.5	24.9	47.5	34.1	62.5	43.2
3.0	6.9	18.0	16.1	33.0	25.2	48.0	34.4	63.0	43.5
3.5	7.2	18.5	16.4	33.5	25.5	48.5	34.7	63.5	43.8
4.0	7.5	19.0	16.7	34.0	25.8	49.0	35.0	64.0	44.1
4.5	7.8	19.5	17.0	34.5	26.1	49.5	35.3	64.5	44.4
5.0	8.2	20.0	17.3	35.0	26.5	50.0	35.6	65.0	44.8
5.5	8.5	20.5	17.6	35.5	26.8	50.5	35.9	65.5	45.1
6.0	8.8	21.0	17.9	36.0	27.1	51.0	36.2	66.0	45.4
6.5	9.1	21.5	18.2	36.5	27.4	51.5	36.5	66.5	45.7
7.0	9.4	22.0	18.5	37.0	27.7	52.0	36.8	67.0	46.0
7.5	9.7	22.5	18.8	37.5	28.0	52.5	37.1	67.5	46.3
8.0	10.0	23.0	19.1	38.0	28.3	53.0	37.4	68.0	46.6
8.5	10.3	23.5	19.4	38.5	28.6	53.5	37.7	68.5	46.9
9.0	10.6	24.0	19.7	39.0	28.9	54.0	38.0	69.0	47.2
9.5	10.9	24.5	20.0	39.5	29.2	54.5	38.3	69.5	47.5
10.0	11.2	25.0	20.4	40.0	29.5	55.0	38.7	70.0	47.8
10.5	11.5	25.5	20.7	40.5	29.8	55.5	39.0	70.5	48.1
11.0	11.8	26.0	21.0	41.0	30.1	56.0	39.3	71.0	48.4
11.5	12.1	26.5	21.3	41.5	30.4	56.5	39.6	71.5	48.7
12.0	12.4	27.0	21.6	42.0	30.7	57.0	39.9	72.0	49.0
12.5	12.7	27.5	21.9	42.5	31.0	57.5	40.2	72.5	49.3
13.0	13.0	28.0	22.2	43.0	31.3	58.0	40.5	73.0	49.6
13.5	13.3	28.5	22.5	43.5	31.6	58.5	40.8	73.5	49.9
14.0	13.6	29.0	22.8	44.0	31.9	59.0	41.1	74.0	50.2
14.5	13.9	29.5	23.1	44.5	32.2	59.5	41.4	74.5	50.5
15.0	14.3	30.0	23.4	45.0	32.6	60.0	41.7	75.0	50.9
15.5	14.6	30.5	23.7	45.5	32.9	60.5	42.0	75.5	51.2

From _FITNESSGRAM/ACTIVITYGRAM Test Administration Manual, Updated Fourth Edition_ by The Cooper Institute, 2010, Champaign, IL: Human Kinetics.

FITNESSGRAM

Class Score Sheet

Teacher _____

Page number _____ Grade _____

Class _____

Test date _____

ID#	Name	Birth date	Sex	Height	Weight	Aerobic capacity ___	Curl-up	Upper body ___	Trunk lift	Flexibility L/R	Skinfolds Triceps	Calf

FIGURE B.11

From *FITNESSGRAM/ACTIVITYGRAM Test Administration Manual, Updated Fourth Edition* by The Cooper Institute, 2010, Champaign, IL: Human Kinetics.

FITNESSGRAM

Personal Fitness Record

Name _____ Age _____ Height _____ School _____ Weight _____ Grade _____

	Date:			Date:			Date:		
	Score	HFZ		Score	HFZ		Score	HFZ	
Aerobic capacity:									
Curl-up									
Trunk lift									
Upper body strength:									
Flexibility:									
Skinfolds:									
Triceps									
Calf									
Total									

Note: HFZ indicates you have performed in the Healthy Fitness Zone.

I understand that my fitness record is personal. I do not have to share my results. My fitness record is important since it allows me to check my fitness level. If it is low, I will need to do more activity. If it is acceptable, I need to continue my current activity level. I know that I can ask my teacher for ideas for improving my fitness level.

FIGURE B.12

From *FITNESSGRAM/ACTIVITYGRAM Test Administration Manual, Updated Fourth Edition* by The Cooper Institute, 2010, Champaign, IL: Human Kinetics.

FITNESSGRAM

Personal Fitness Record

Name _____ Age _____ Height _____ School _____ Weight _____ Grade _____

	Date:			Date:			Date:		
	Score	HFZ		Score	HFZ		Score	HFZ	
Aerobic capacity:									
Curl-up									
Trunk lift									
Upper body strength:									
Flexibility:									
Skinfolds:									
Triceps									
Calf									
Total									

Note: HFZ indicates you have performed in the Healthy Fitness Zone.

I understand that my fitness record is personal. I do not have to share my results. My fitness record is important since it allows me to check my fitness level. If it is low, I will need to do more activity. If it is acceptable, I need to continue my current activity level. I know that I can ask my teacher for ideas for improving my fitness level.

FIGURE B.12

From *FITNESSGRAM/ACTIVITYGRAM Test Administration Manual, Updated Fourth Edition* by The Cooper Institute, 2010, Champaign, IL: Human Kinetics.

FITNESSGRAM

Personal Fitness Record

Name _____ School _____ Grade _____ Age _____ Ht _____ Wt _____

	Date:		Date:		Date:	
	Score	HFZ	Score	HFZ	Score	HFZ
Aerobic capacity: _____						
Curl-up						
Trunk lift						
Upper body strength: _____						
Flexibility: _____						
Skinfolds:						
Triceps						
Calf						
Total						

Note: HFZ indicates you have performed in the Healthy Fitness Zone.

I understand that my fitness record is personal. I do not have to share my results. My fitness record is important since it allows me to check my fitness level. If it is low, I will need to do more activity. If it is acceptable, I need to continue my current activity level. I know that I can ask my teacher for ideas for improving my fitness level.

FIGURE B.13

From *FITNESSGRAM/ACTIVITYGRAM Test Administration Manual, Updated Fourth Edition* by The Cooper Institute, 2010, Champaign, IL: Human Kinetics.

FITNESSGRAM

Personal Fitness Record

Name _____ School _____ Grade _____ Age _____ Ht _____ Wt _____

	Date:		Date:		Date:	
	Score	HFZ	Score	HFZ	Score	HFZ
Aerobic capacity: _____						
Curl-up						
Trunk lift						
Upper body strength: _____						
Flexibility: _____						
Skinfolds:						
Triceps						
Calf						
Total						

Note: HFZ indicates you have performed in the Healthy Fitness Zone.

I understand that my fitness record is personal. I do not have to share my results. My fitness record is important since it allows me to check my fitness level. If it is low, I will need to do more activity. If it is acceptable, I need to continue my current activity level. I know that I can ask my teacher for ideas for improving my fitness level.

FIGURE B.13

From *FITNESSGRAM/ACTIVITYGRAM Test Administration Manual, Updated Fourth Edition* by The Cooper Institute, 2010, Champaign, IL: Human Kinetics.

FITNESSGRAM

ACTIVITYGRAM Assessment—Sample Log

Name _____ Teacher _____ Grade _____ Date _____

Record the main activity that you did during each 30-minute time period by writing the activity type and activity number in the appropriate box (types and numbers can be found in the box located at the bottom of the page). You may have done many things in each 30-minute time period, but try to pick the activity you did for most of the time. Then, check the box that describes how it felt (light/easy (**L**), moderate/medium (**M**), vigorous/hard (**V**)). Note: for all rest activities, use the **Rest** box and you can leave the L, M, or V columns blank. In the Time column, write the amount of time that the activity felt this hard or easy: **S** (some), **M** (most), or **A** (all).

Time	Type	Number	Rest	L	M	V	Time	Time	Type	Number	Rest	L	M	V	Time
7:00	LA	5	X				A	3:00							
7:30	LA	5	X				A	3:30							
8:00	LA	5	X				A	4:00							
8:30	LA	2			X		M	4:30							
9:00	AA	8				X	M	5:00							
9:30	LA	25		X			S	5:30							
10:00								6:00							
10:30								6:30							
11:00								7:00							
11:30								7:30							
12:00								8:00							
12:30								8:30							
1:00								9:00							
1:30								9:30							
2:00								10:00							
2:30								10:30							

Activity Types and Numbers

Lifestyle activity (LA)	Aerobic sports (AE)	Flexibility activity (FA)
1. Walk, bike, skate	11. Field sports	21. Martial arts
2. Housework/yardwork	12. Court sports	22. Stretching
3. Active games/play	13. Racket sports	23. Yoga
4. Active job	14. Aerobic sports–PE	24. Ballet dance
5. Other lifestyle activity	15. Other aerobic sports	25. Other flexibility
Aerobic activity (AA)	**Muscular activity (MA)**	**Resting (R)**
6. Aerobic class/dancing	16. Gymnastics	26. Schoolwork
7. Aerobic gym	17. Muscular sports	27. Computer/TV
8. Aerobic activity	18. Weightlifting	28. Eating/resting
9. Aerobic activity in PE	19. Wrestling	29. Sleeping
10. Other aerobic activity	20. Other muscular	30. Other rest

FIGURE B.14

From *FITNESSGRAM/ACTIVITYGRAM Test Administration Manual, Updated Fourth Edition* by The Cooper Institute, 2010, Champaign, IL: Human Kinetics.

FITNESSGRAM

ACTIVITYGRAM Assessment—Day 1 2 3

Name _____ Teacher _____ Grade _____ Date _____

Record the main activity that you did during each 30-minute time period by writing the activity type and activity number in the appropriate box (types and numbers can be found in the box located at the bottom of the page). You may have done many things in each 30-minute time period, but try to pick the activity you did for most of the time. Then, check the box that describes how it felt (light/easy (**L**), moderate/medium (**M**), vigorous/hard (**V**)). Note: for all rest activities, use the **Rest** box and you can leave the L, M, or V columns blank. In the Time column, write the amount of time that the activity felt this hard or easy: **S** (some), **M** (most), or **A** (all).

Time	Type	Number	Rest	L	M	V	Time	Time	Type	Number	Rest	L	M	V	Time
7:00								3:00							
7:30								3:30							
8:00								4:00							
8:30								4:30							
9:00								5:00							
9:30								5:30							
10:00								6:00							
10:30								6:30							
11:00								7:00							
11:30								7:30							
12:00								8:00							
12:30								8:30							
1:00								9:00							
1:30								9:30							
2:00								10:00							
2:30								10:30							

Activity Types and Numbers

Lifestyle activity (LA)	Aerobic sports (AE)	Flexibility activity (FA)
1. Walk, bike, skate	11. Field sports	21. Martial arts
2. Housework/yardwork	12. Court sports	22. Stretching
3. Active games/play	13. Racket sports	23. Yoga
4. Active job	14. Aerobic sports–PE	24. Ballet dance
5. Other lifestyle activity	15. Other aerobic sports	25. Other flexibility
Aerobic activity (AA)	**Muscular activity (MA)**	**Resting (R)**
6. Aerobic class/dancing	16. Gymnastics	26. Schoolwork
7. Aerobic gym	17. Muscular sports	27. Computer/TV
8. Aerobic activity	18. Weightlifting	28. Eating/resting
9. Aerobic activity in PE	19. Wrestling	29. Sleeping
10. Other aerobic activity	20. Other muscular	30. Other rest

FIGURE B.15

From *FITNESSGRAM/ACTIVITYGRAM Test Administration Manual, Updated Fourth Edition* by The Cooper Institute, 2010, Champaign, IL: Human Kinetics.

HEALTH-RELATED FITNESS TRACKING CHARTS—COPY MASTERS

FITNESSGRAM®

Boy's
Health-Related Fitness
Tracking Charts

From *FITNESSGRAM/ACTIVITYGRAM Test Administration Manual, Updated Fourth Edition* by The Cooper Institute, 2010, Champaign, IL: Human Kinetics.

Student   School

From FITNESSGRAM/ACTIVITYGRAM Test Administration Manual, Updated Fourth Edition by The Cooper Institute, 2010, Champaign, IL: Human Kinetics.

How to Use

FITNESSGRAM Longitudinal Tracking Chart is to be used to chart the fitness level of each individual from the first *FITNESSGRAM* testing experience to the last. There is a graph for every test item to be used in plotting the scores for each test date. The gray shaded area in the graph indicates the Healthy Fitness Zone for that test item (unless otherwise specified). Use this chart in addition to the *FITNESSGRAM* report to communicate long-term progress in maintaining healthy fitness levels.

Follow these simple instructions:

1. Write the child's name on the front of the chart in the space provided.

2. Mark the current score for each test on the appropriate graph. It is suggested that a distinctive mark that is easy to make such as ■, ■, or ✱ be used.

3. At the next test date, mark the score with the same symbol. Draw a line connecting the two marks.

4. Notice that the minor mark is included on the X-axis indicating six-month intervals to use if testing is conducted twice during a school year.

5. The graphs for height and weight indicate the 5th, 50th, and 95th percentile levels for growth.

Here is an example:

Boy's Curl-Up Example

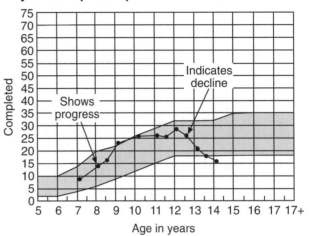

Other Suggestions

■ Use the graphs to chart the progress for an entire school district by using the mean scores from the Statistical Summary Report. These reports can be produced with the *FITNESSGRAM* software program.

■ Allow children to complete their own charts and integrate this activity into math class.

Aerobic Capacity

Boy's Aerobic Capacity

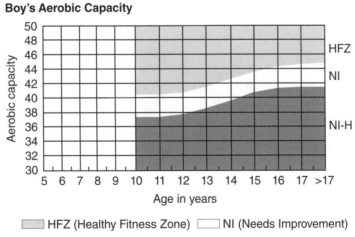

Muscle Strength, Endurance, and Flexibility

Boy's Curl-Ups

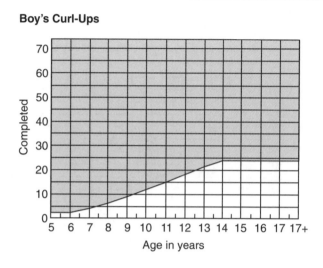

Boy's Trunk Lift

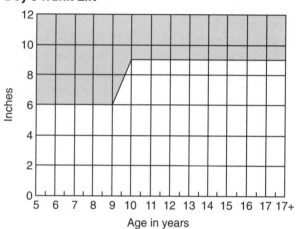

Boy's Push-Ups

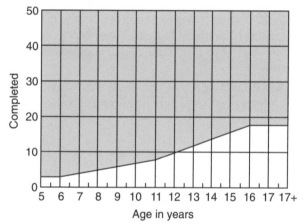

Boy's Modified Pull-Ups

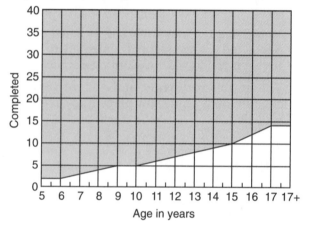

Boy's Flexed Arm Hang

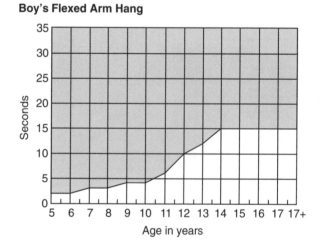

Boy's Back-Saver Sit and Reach

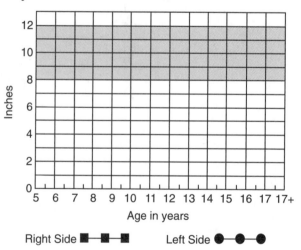

Right Side ■—■—■   Left Side ●—●—●

From *FITNESSGRAM/ACTIVITYGRAM Test Administration Manual, Updated Fourth Edition* by The Cooper Institute, 2010, Champaign, IL: Human Kinetics.

Body Size and Body Composition

From *FITNESSGRAM/ACTIVITYGRAM Test Administration Manual, Updated Fourth Edition* by The Cooper Institute, 2010, Champaign, IL: Human Kinetics.

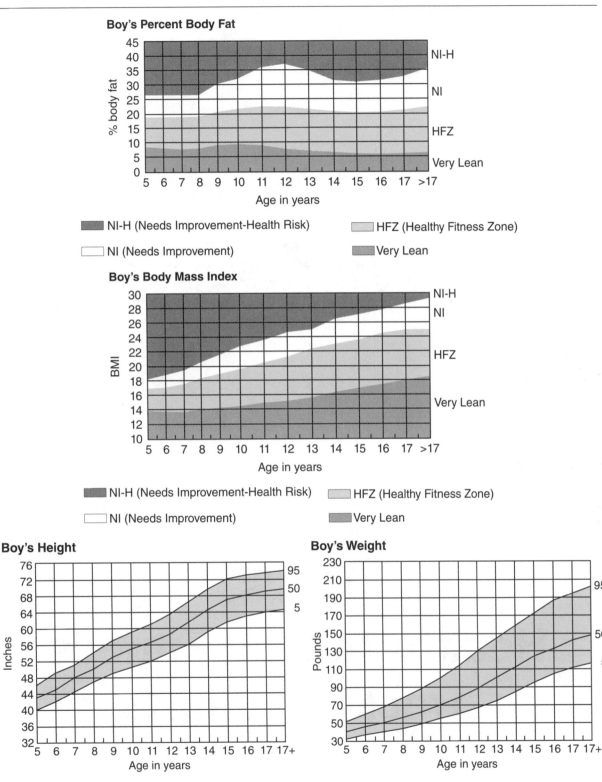

© 1994, 1999, 2004, 2005, 2007, 2010 The Cooper Institute.
Developed by The Cooper Institute, Dallas, Texas. Endorsed by The American Alliance for Health, Physical Education, Recreation and Dance.
All rights reserved. School districts and youth agencies have permission to reproduce any part of this chart for use within the local school district or youth agency only.
Height and weight charts adapted from the National Center for Health Statistics and National Center for Chronic Disease Prevention and Health Promotion, 2000. www.cdc.gov/growthcharts

FITNESSGRAM®

Girl's
Health-Related Fitness
Tracking Charts

From *FITNESSGRAM/ACTIVITYGRAM Test Administration Manual, Updated Fourth Edition* by The Cooper Institute, 2010, Champaign, IL: Human Kinetics.

Student   School

From *FITNESSGRAM/ACTIVITYGRAM Test Administration Manual, Updated Fourth Edition* by The Cooper Institute, 2010, Champaign, IL: Human Kinetics.

How to Use

FITNESSGRAM Longitudinal Tracking Chart is to be used to chart the fitness level of each individual from the first *FITNESSGRAM* testing experience to the last. There is a graph for every test item to be used in plotting the scores for each test date. The gray shaded area in the graph indicates the Healthy Fitness Zone for that test item (unless otherwise specified). Use this chart in addition to the *FITNESSGRAM* report to communicate long-term progress in maintaining healthy fitness levels.

Follow these simple instructions:

1. Write the child's name on the front of the chart in the space provided.

2. Mark the current score for each test on the appropriate graph. It is suggested that a distinctive mark that is easy to make such as ■, ■, or * be used.

3. At the next test date, mark the score with the same symbol. Draw a line connecting the two marks.

4. Notice that the minor mark is included on the X-axis indicating six-month intervals to use if testing is conducted twice during a school year.

5. The graphs for height and weight indicate the 5th, 50th, and 95th percentile levels for growth.

Here is an example:

Girl's Curl-Up Example

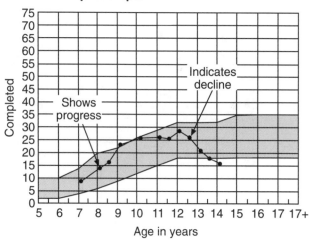

Other Suggestions

■ Use the graphs to chart the progress for an entire school district by using the mean scores from the Statistical Summary Report. These reports can be produced with the *FITNESSGRAM* software program.

■ Allow children to complete their own charts and integrate this activity into math class.

Aerobic Capacity

Girl's Aerobic Capacity

HFZ (Healthy Fitness Zone) ☐ NI (Needs Improvement)
NI-H (Needs Improvement-Health Risk)

Muscle Strength, Endurance, and Flexibility

Girl's Curl-Ups

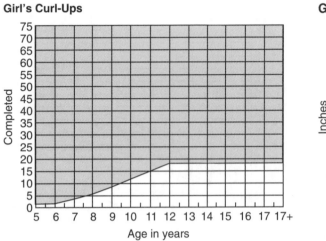

Girl's Trunk Lift

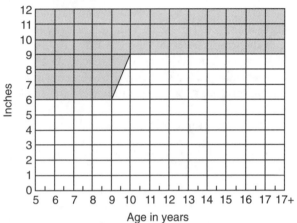

Girl's Push-Ups

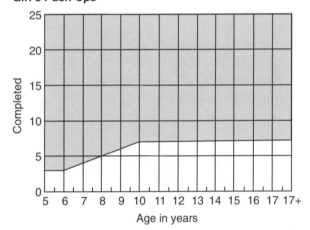

Girl's Modified Pull-Ups

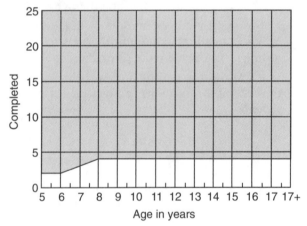

Girl's Flexed Arm Hang

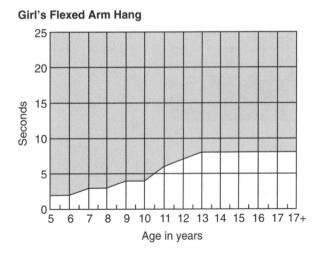

Girl's Back-Saver Sit and Reach

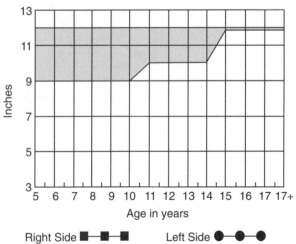

Right Side ■—■—■   Left Side ●—●—●

From *FITNESSGRAM/ACTIVITYGRAM Test Administration Manual, Updated Fourth Edition* by The Cooper Institute, 2010, Champaign, IL: Human Kinetics.

Body Size and Body Composition

From *FITNESSGRAM/ACTIVITYGRAM Test Administration Manual, Updated Fourth Edition* by The Cooper Institute, 2010, Champaign, IL: Human Kinetics.

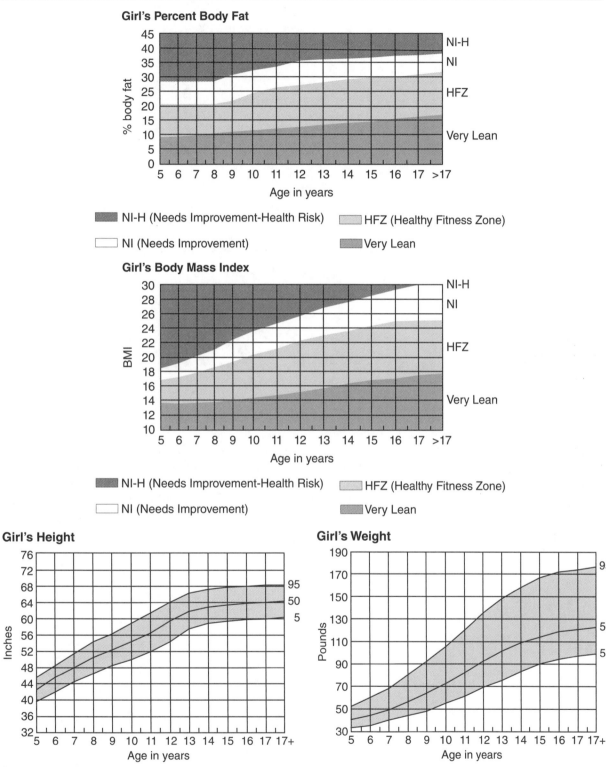

Girl's Percent Body Fat

Girl's Body Mass Index

Girl's Height

Girl's Weight

© 1994, 1999, 2004, 2005, 2007, 2010 The Cooper Institute.

Developed by The Cooper Institute, Dallas, Texas. Endorsed by The American Alliance for Health, Physical Education, Recreation and Dance.

All rights reserved. School districts and youth agencies have permission to reproduce any part of this chart for use within the local school district or youth agency only.

Height and weight charts adapted from the National Center for Health Statistics and National Center for Chronic Disease Prevention and Health Promotion, 2000. www.cdc.gov/growthcharts

FAQS

The *FITNESSGRAM* Web site at www.Fitnessgram. net features lists of frequently asked questions (FAQs) for multiple audiences. Click on the FAQs button on the home page to find answers to the most common questions asked by parents, teachers, and technical staff.

The Parent FAQs are available in English *or Spanish*. The technical FAQs cover general tech questions, plus questions specific to each version of the *FITNESSGRAM* software.

There's also a list of the top 10 questions people ask about *FITNESSGRAM* when they're considering a purchase of *FITNESSGRAM* software.

SOFTWARE USER MANUAL

Contents

About the FITNESSGRAM Software

There are two releases of the *FITNESSGRAM* software: *FITNESSGRAM* 8 and *FITNESSGRAM* 9.

FITNESSGRAM 8

The *FITNESSGRAM* 8 program is client-based software and is available in three versions. For specific and updated system requirements for each version, please go to the FITNESSGRAM Web site (www.fitnessgram.net) and click the Technical Assistance button.

1. Stand Alone: This is for Windows or Macintosh computers. Program is not networkable and has to be installed to individual computers.
2. Small Area Network: This program is installed within a LAN environment for one site or building only. A Windows server must be used, but the individual clients can be Windows or Macs.
3. District SQL: This program is for use over a wide-area network with many sites or buildings. System requirements specify a SQL server for the database with the client installations either Windows or Macs.

Licensing

The *FITNESSGRAM* 8 software is included in each *FITNESSGRAM* Test Kit along with licensing information. Accompanying each kit are abbreviated installation instructions and an information sheet with step-by-step instructions on using your invoice number to obtain a license file needed for installation of the FG 8 program. For complete installation instructions, please review the Readme file located on your software CD.

Software Training Videos for FITNESSGRAM 8

Software training videos have been developed for the FG 8 program. The license agreement for using the videos is very liberal. Place it on your network or intranet or duplicate to CDs and hand out to teachers using the program. The videos are located in these areas for ease of use:

- On each software CD
- On the *FITNESSGRAM* manual DVD
- On the www.fitnessgram.net Web site under the Training button

FITNESSGRAM 9

The latest release of the *FITNESSGRAM* program is Web based and is available in three versions. For specific and updated system requirements for each version as well as other technical information, please go to the FITNESSGRAM Web site (www.fitnessgram.net) and click the Technical Assistance button.

1. State and Large Metro: For states and large metropolitan districts wanting to conduct fitness data collection on a wide scale
2. District: For two or more schools in a district
3. School: For one school in a district

There is no Stand Alone FG 9 program. If you want a single installation of *FITNESSGRAM,* then you will need to use the *FITNESSGRAM* 8 Stand Alone software, which is not a Web-based product and is not networkable.

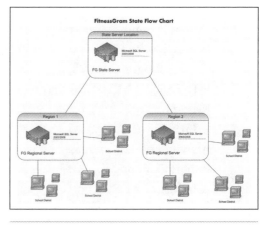

FIGURE E.1   Flow of information for the FG 9 State and Large Metro Program.

Licensing

The *FITNESSGRAM* 9 program is downloaded from the FG Web site and is not included in the Test Kit. A license key is provided with the number of school, site, or building licenses available from your purchase. Instructions are also included regarding use of the license key with your program. With the license key, you control the number of site licenses available to you. Thus, you can change school names or delete and add when schools are no longer in service and when a new one comes on board. To add a school, site, or building to an existing license key, please contact your sales rep.

Technical Support for Both FITNESSGRAM 8 and 9 Programs

On the FITNESSGRAM Web site (www.fitnessgram.net) are many technical documents (i.e., data management) as well as installation instructions and system requirements for the *FITNESSGRAM* 8 and *FITNESSGRAM* 9 programs. Please review with school or district IT staff when considering your next FG program.

Contact Human Kinetics technical support using any one of these methods:

- E-mail: support@hkusa.com
- Phone: 800-747-4457, option #3
- Fax: 217-351-2674

When talking with Human Kinetics technical support staff, please provide the following:

1. Which software program you are using (either *FITNESSGRAM* 8 or 9) and the correct version
2. If there is an error message, the exact wording of the message
3. A complete description of what happened and what you were doing when the error message appeared
4. An explanation of how you tried to troubleshoot the problem

Online Training Course for FITNESSGRAM

A free online training course is available based on the *FITNESSGRAM* manual. Locate it on the FG Web site (www.fitnessgram.net) under the Training button.

Instructions for FITNESSGRAM 8 and FITNESSGRAM 9 Software Programs

In this section of the *FITNESSGRAM* manual, only abbreviated and basic instructions are provided for the *FITNESSGRAM* 8 (FG 8) and *FITNESSGRAM* 9 (FG 9) software programs. Differences are noted where applicable. For more detailed information on entering data into the programs, please review the extensive Help files in each program or the FITNESSGRAM Web site (www.fitnessgram.net).

Note that FG 9 is the latest release of the *FITNESSGRAM* program. Thus, there are many features in FG 9 that are not present in FG 8. These differences are noted in this section.

In addition to the *FITNESSGRAM* fitness assessment in the software, there are two activity modules:

1. ACTIVITYGRAM is an activity assessment where students enter their activity behaviors over a three-day period.
2. Activity Log is where students enter their pedometer steps and/or minutes of activity.

The *FITNESSGRAM* computer program has two applications: the Teacher program and the Student program. In the student application, students enter their FITNESSGRAM, ACTIVITYGRAM, and Activity Log scores.

Teacher Program

It's easy to move around in the *FITNESSGRAM* program and to get from one screen to another. In each instance you or your IT staff will need to establish the data relationships of district, school, teacher, class, and student before you can enter FITNESSGRAM results.

To access the program after installation, do the following:

- FG 8: Double-click on the FG 8 Teacher icon on your desktop (Windows users) or docking bar (Mac users).

- FG 9: Use your single sign-on account or type in the URL for your FITNESSGRAM Web site. Log in accordingly.

Getting Started

Whether you are using FG 8 or FG 9, before you can enter FG or AG data, you will need to establish the teacher, class, and student relationships in the program. You can do this either by manually entering this information or importing from your district or school databases into the program. If you will import this information, carefully read through the technical documents within the software or on the FITNESS-GRAM Web site.

Adding Teachers

In both programs, teachers have to be entered by someone with a high security level (i.e., school or district administrator) or via an import. Once teachers and their logins have been created, then you can start working in the program. Please contact a school or district administrator or a member of your IT staff for your login (user name and password) to the program.

Entering Teacher Information

For both the FG 8 and FG 9 programs, all teachers must be entered into the software before they can access the program. You can do this either manually or via an import. Instructions for manually entering all teachers using the program are provided here. To import, please read the technical documents on the FG Web site.

Edit Teacher Information

Teachers can edit only their own information.

FG 8

1. Click on the Teacher icon.

2. Highlight your name in the list box.

3. Make the edits as needed and click the OK button.

FG 9

1. Click on My Info at top right of the screen.

2. Make the edits as needed and click the OK button.

Delete Teacher Information

Only individuals with a higher security level can delete a teacher or change a teacher's security level.

Entering Class Information

Once teachers have been added to the FG program, you will need to create classes for each teacher.

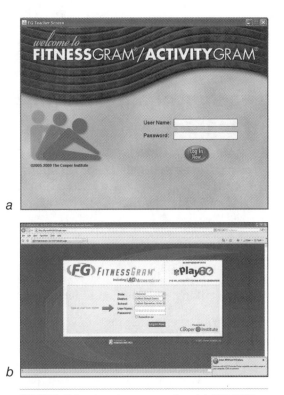

a

b

FIGURE E.2   Log-in screens for (a) FITNESS-GRAM 8 and (b) FITNESSGRAM 9.

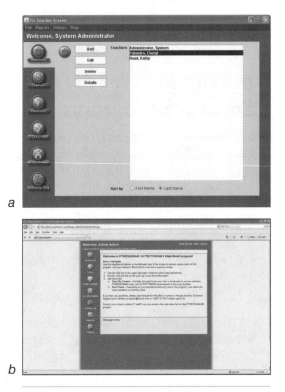

a

b

FIGURE E.3   Teacher screens for (a) FG 8 and (b) FG 9.

Add a Class

FG 8

1. Click on the Classes icon. Make sure that your name as teacher is visible on screen.
2. Click the Add button.
3. Enter in class name and click the OK button. Repeat as needed until all classes are entered.

FG 9

1. Click the My Classes icon. Make sure that your name as teacher is visible on screen.
2. Click the Add button.
3. Enter in class name and other information as needed, and click the OK button. Repeat as needed until all classes are entered.

Note: Some FG 9 customers may not have permission to add a class name. Please check with your district administrator or IT staff if you do not have permission to add, edit, or delete a class name.

Edit a Class

1. Click on Classes (FG 8) or My Classes (FG 9) icon. Make sure your name as teacher is visible on screen.
2. Select the Edit button (FG 8) or check the box next to the class (FG 9) and click the Edit button.
3. Make the necessary corrections.

Note: Some FG 9 customers may not have permission to edit a class name. Please check with your district administrator or IT staff if you do not have permission to add, edit, or delete a class name.

Delete a Class

1. Click on Classes (FG 8) or My Classes (FG 9) icon.
2. Select the Delete button (FG 8) or check the box next to the class (FG 9) and click the Delete button.
3. Both FG programs will verify that you do want to delete the class.

Note: Some FG 9 customers may not have permission to delete a class name.

Entering Student Information

Create students once classes have been entered into the software. Students can be entered manually or through an import. Instructions here are for manual entry of student information. Please review the technical documents in your program's Help files or online via the FG Web site.

Add a Student

FG 8

1. Click on the Students icon.
2. Click the Add button.
3. Enter in all relevant student information (the following are required fields in order to calculate FG results) and click the OK button. Repeat as needed until all students are entered.
   a. Student name
   b. Student ID/Number
   c. Grade
   d. Gender
   e. Date of birth
   f. Optional information
      i. Student user name and password (for students to use the Student application to enter data for FG, AG, and AL)
      ii. Student nickname
      iii. Ethnicity

4. Print body composition: By default, body composition information is displayed on FG student and parent reports. If you do not want to print BC information for a specific student, then uncheck the box.
5. Print the report in Spanish: By default, the student and parent FG reports are printed in English. If you want to print these reports in Spanish for a specific student, then check the box.

FG 9

1. Click the My Classes icon.
2. Click the link for Add Students.
3. Enter in all relevant student information (following are required fields in order to calculate FG results) and click the OK button. Repeat as needed until all students are entered.
   a. Student name
   b. Student ID/Number
   c. Grade
   d. Gender
   e. Date of birth
   f. Optional information
      i. Student user name and password (for students to use the Student application to enter data for FG, AG, and AL)
      ii. Student nickname
      iii. Ethnicity
      iv. E-mail addresses for student and parent or guardian
      v. Home mailing address
4. Print body composition: By default, body composition information is displayed on FG student and parent reports. If you do not want to print BC information for a specific student, then uncheck the box.
5. Print the report in Spanish: By default, the student and parent FG reports are printed in English. If you want to print these reports in Spanish for a specific student, then check the box.

Note: Some FG 9 customers may not have permission to manually add students.

Edit a Student

1. Click on Students (FG 8) or My Classes (FG 9) icon.
2. Select the Edit button (FG 8). For FG 9, select Edit students (FG 9), check the box next to the student, and click the Edit button.
3. Make the necessary corrections.

Note: Some FG 9 customers may not have permission to edit a class name.

Delete a Student

1. Click on Classes (FG 8) or My Classes (FG 9) icon.
2. Select the Delete button (FG 8). For FG 9, check the box next to the student and click the Delete button.
3. Both FG programs will verify that you want to delete the class.

Note: Some FG 9 customers may not have permission to delete a student.

Notes

1. Required fields are marked with an asterisk (*) (e.g., last name and first name).
2. Body composition information, by default, is printed on FG student and parent reports. To not print body composition information, please follow these steps:
   a. For individual students, go into the student record and uncheck the Print Body Comp box.
   b. For an entire class, go into the FG test event and uncheck the Print Body Comp box.
3. If you do not include a student number or ID when adding a student (either by manually creating the student or through an import), the program will automatically create and assign a number.

4. The ethnicity field is optional in FG 8 but may be optional or required in FG 9. Check with your district or state if this information is needed when reporting student FG results to a state agency.

5. Students can also be added or edited via the student Details button.

Entering Student Logins (User Names and Passwords)

For both FG 8 and FG 9, if students are using the student application to enter FITNESSGRAM, ACTIVITY-GRAM, or Activity Log information, you can create the logins either manually or via the import process. If user names and passwords are not entered through either method, the FG program will automatically create them for the student.

FITNESSGRAM Tests and Scores

Once you have created all the necessary data relationships (i.e., teachers, classes, and students), you can create FITNESSGRAM test events and enter FG scores. For either the FG 8 or FG 9 programs, click on the FITNESSGRAM icon.

Add a FG Test Event

1. Click the Add button.

2. Enter the name of the test event. Be descriptive, such as Fall Pretest or Spring Posttest. Do not enter the name of a specific test item as a test event name.

3. Select a date for the test event.

4. Print body composition. By default, body composition information is displayed on FG student and parent reports. If you do not want to print BC information for this test event and class, uncheck the box.

5. Print the report in Spanish. By default, the student and parent FG reports are printed in English. If for this test event you want these reports printed in Spanish, check the box.

6. Select the test items for the test event:

   a. Aerobic Capacity: Select PACER, Mile Run, or the Walk Test.

   b. Body Composition: Enter skinfold measurements (triceps and calf), percent body fat from a BIA device, or height and weight values for calculation of body mass index.

   c. Select Muscular Strength, Endurance, or Flexibility test items.

      i. Curl-up and Trunk Lift are mandatory test items for FG.

      ii. Select Push-up, Modified Pull-up, or Flexed Arm Hang.

      iii. Select Back-Saver Sit-and-Reach or Shoulder Stretch.

   d. Select activity days: Keep same text.

Note: In FG 9 a PE administrator can mandate the test items teachers are to use when testing students.

Edit a Test Event

1. Accessing the FG icon, highlight the test event to edit (FG 8) or check the box of the test event (FG 9).

2. Make the necessary corrections and click OK.

3. Note in FG 9 that a teacher may not have permission to edit a test event.

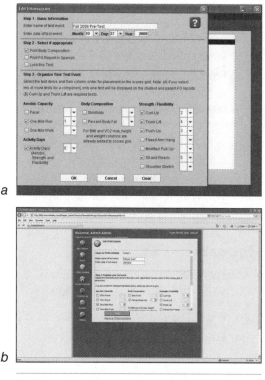

a

b

FIGURE E.4 How to create a FG test event for *(a)* FG 8 and *(b)* FG 9.

Delete a Test Event

1. Accessing the FG icon, highlight the test event to delete (FG 8) or check the box of the test event (FG 9).
2. Click the Delete button.
3. Note in FG 9 that a teacher may not have permission to delete a test event.

Entering FG Test Scores

1. Accessing the FG icon, highlight the test event (FG 8) or check the box of the test event (FG 9) and click the Scores button.
2. Enter test scores for your students.
3. Use the tab or arrow keys to navigate from field to field.

Notes

- If you prefer, you can print a score sheet from the Reports menu icon or the scores screen to enter scores by hand, then transfer to the software. To print from the scores screen, click the Scores button. At the bottom of the screen, click the Print Scores Sheet button.
- If you do not want body composition information and test results printed on the FITNESSGRAM student and parent reports, uncheck the Print Body Composition box for the test event.
- If you want the FITNESSGRAM reports to be printed in Spanish, check the box.
- If you have students enter their test scores from the student program, their test results will be accessible within the teacher program and can be viewed via the Scores button.
- If you have students enter scores from the student program for tests you generated from the teacher program,

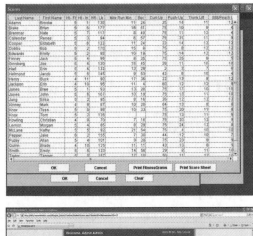

FIGURE E.5 How to enter scores for (a) FG 8 and (b) FG 9.

you can lock the test so that test scores cannot be changed once entered. Check the Lock This Test box.
- Students can create their own tests within the student program. These test results are also transferred to the teacher program. On the teacher main screen, check the Show Student-Generated Test Records box. All student-generated tests from the student program will be displayed by the student's last name and date of test. These tests cannot be locked.
- A FITNESSGRAM student report can also be generated from the Scores screen. Select the Print FITNESSGRAM button to print test results for that test.
- Gender, grade, and date of birth are column headings within the scores screen. If these are not entered, you will be unable to print a report for that student.
- To enter test scores using a PDA, consult the Help files within the program.

Reports

A variety of reports are available from FG 8 and FG 9 and all are printed in PDF using Adobe Acrobat Reader. To access the reports, do the following:

- For FG 8, go to the Reports menu and select the Report Wizard.
- For FG 9, click the Reports Icon.

Steps

1. Depending on your security level, license, and software version purchased, select one of the options from the drop-down lists.

2. At the next screen, make your selections based on displayed options.

3. Reports for your selections will be displayed. Note that several reports have options concerning how information is displayed.

4. For complete information on printing reports and all available options, please read the Help files.

Report Options

- FITNESSGRAM Student Report: This report displays the student's fitness test scores, the relationship of the scores to the Healthy Fitness Zone, and information on how to improve or maintain current fitness levels.

- FITNESSGRAM Student Information Back Page: This static page speaks directly to the student.

- FITNESSGRAM Parent Report: Report to be sent home to parents explaining *FITNESSGRAM* tests and the Healthy Fitness Zone. All test results are displayed using the Healthy Fitness Zone.

- FITNESSGRAM Parent Information Page: A separate back page of information for parents on the importance of physical activity for children and their families.

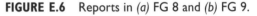

FIGURE E.6   Reports in (a) FG 8 and (b) FG 9.

- FITNESSGRAM Score Sheet: Prints a score sheet for a FITNESSGRAM test event to record scores.

- FITNESSGRAM Longitudinal Tracking Report: Tracks and plots the students' scores on FITNESSGRAM test items through their school careers. A second option is to print a blank report that teachers can use for students to graph their scores.

- FITNESSGRAM Self-Assessment Data Sheet: A blank score sheet that students can use to write down their FITNESSGRAM test scores during the testing process.

- FITNESSGRAM Statistics Report: Contains group summary information, including mean, standard deviation, range of scores, and percentage of students achieving the Healthy Fitness Zone by test item, age, and gender.

- Achievement of Standards Report: List of students achieving the Healthy Fitness Zone for a specified number of test items or for a specific test item.

- Student Information Report: Lists student name, ID, user name, and password for the student program.

- Summary Report: Summary of all test results for selected classes and students.

- Student Certificate: Generates a recognition certificate for selected students. The certificate is personalized with the student's name and reason for achievement.

- ACTIVITYGRAM Information Page: Teachers inform students about the importance of being physically active.

- ACTIVITYGRAM Student Report: Provides results from student-entered activity levels for a two- or three-day period. It can also be printed from the student program.

- ACTIVITYGRAM Self-Assessment Data Sheet: A blank activity sheet that students can use to select those activities matching their physical activity level or over a two- or three-day period.

- ACTIVITYGRAM Statistics Report: Two ACTIVITYGRAM reports provide statistics for minutes of activity within the activity categories and overall minutes of activity for a two- or three-day time period.

- Activity Log Student Individual Report: Also printed from the student program, this report tracks daily entries for pedometer steps and minutes of physical activity and determines total amount of steps and minutes for a specified time period and a daily average. A second option is to print a blank form for students so they can enter daily pedometer steps or minutes of physical activity.
- Activity Log PALA Eligibility Report: This is for the Presidential Active Lifestyle Award. Teachers print this to determine students who are eligible to receive the award for a given amount of steps or minutes.
- Activity Log Summary Report: This report details student and class statistics on pedometer steps and minutes of physical activity.
- Data Validation: This report lists those students who do not have a date of birth, grade, gender, or ethnicity entered. It also provides information on teachers not assigned to a school.

In FG 9, these reports are also included and are not available in FG 8:

- Exemptions report: Use this report to view reasons why some students did not participate in testing (e.g., injury, disability, absence).
- FG statistical comparison reports achieving the Healthy Fitness Zone by specific test items or by fitness components:
  a. Unit Comparison Report: Lists percentage of boys and girls and totals for one or more schools.
  b. Grade or Range Comparison Report: Lists results by specific grades or by grade range such as elementary, middle, or secondary.
  c. Test or Component Comparison Report: Results are grouped by specific test items or by fitness components.
  d. Achievement of Standards Report: Percentage of students by specific grades or by grade range such as elementary, middle, or secondary by test items or fitness components.

FIGURE E.7   Screen shot of FG Comparison Reports in FG 9.

ACTIVITYGRAM

An easy way to use ACTIVITYGRAM is to create a series of assignments (e.g., monthly or quarterly) so students are more aware of their activity habits. As a teacher, you will be able to view or edit student ACTIVITYGRAM information entered via the student program. In the ACTIVITYGRAM component, students enter the amount and types of activity done over a two- or three-day period.

Teachers can also enter student data and print reports for students. The ACTIVITYGRAM report (accessible via the Reports menu) provides students with feedback on their daily activity levels and informs them if too much time is spent in sedentary activities such as playing video games or watching TV.

Access ACTIVITYGRAM by clicking on the ACTIVITYGRAM icon. You can then add, edit, or delete ACTIVITYGRAM information.

Add an ACTIVITYGRAM Assignment for a Class

1. Click the ACTIVITYGRAM icon. Click the Add (FG8) or Create (FG9) button.
2. Enter the name of the AG event and other information as indicated.

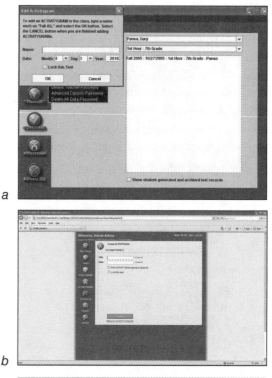

a

b

FIGURE E.8   Creating an ACTIVITYGRAM assignment in *(a)* FG 8 and *(b)* FG 9.

3. Lock the AG: By checking this box once students have entered their activities, students will be able to view their entries but will not be able to edit them.

4. Click OK to save the ACTIVITYGRAM.

Edit an ACTIVITYGRAM

1. Highlight the ACTIVITYGRAM (FG 8) or check the box (FG 9) and click the Edit button.

2. Make any necessary changes and save the changes.

Delete an ACTIVITYGRAM

1. Highlight the ACTIVITYGRAM (FG 8) or check the box (FG 9) and click the Delete button.

2. FITNESSGRAM program will prompt you to make sure you want to delete the AG assignment.

To Print an ACTIVITYGRAM

Go to the Reports pull-down menu (FG 8) or the Reports icon (FG9) to print ACTIVITYGRAM student reports or statistical ACTIVITYGRAM reports for your classes, school, or district.

Activity Log

In the student program, students record their pedometer steps or minutes of activity using the Activity Log. In the teacher program, teachers can view or edit individual student data and can issue challenges for pedometer steps and minutes of activity to other classes or to other schools (depending on the license).

To view, add, or edit student data, do the following:

1. Click on the Activity Log icon.

2. Highlight the student's name in the list box to view, add, or edit data.

3. Enter pedometer steps and minutes of physical activity in the monthly calendar format.

To delete activity log data for a student, do the following:

1. Click on the Activity Log icon.

2. Highlight the student's name in the list box.

3. Click the Delete button. The program will ask if you want to delete that student's activity log. If so, the log entries for that student will be deleted.

Challenges

To create and issue an Activity Log challenge, do the following:

1. Select the Challenges button on the screen.

2. Select the New button from the menu.

3. Enter the name of the challenge.

4. Select the target for the challenge (district, teacher, or class). Then select one or more items in the list box.

5. Enter a brief explanation of the challenge.

6. Enter a challenge goal measured by steps or minutes of activity.

7. Enter a start and end date for the challenge.

8. Click the OK button to save and issue the challenge.

To edit a challenge, do the following:

1. Select the Challenge button. Then, select the Challenge from the list box you would like to edit.

2. Make the edits and click OK to save. Note that any data entered before the edit may be lost.

To delete a challenge, do the following:

1. Select the Challenge button. Then, select the Challenge from the list box you would like to delete.

2. Click the Delete button.

To view challenge standings, do the following:

1. Select the Challenge button, then select Standings.
2. Select the challenge to view current standings for all participants (e.g., schools, classes, and students). You can view totals for steps and minutes of activity along with averages.
3. Use the Expand All or Collapse All buttons to view results within a challenge.

Import Options

Through the Import feature, you can save time by importing teacher, class, or student information as well as historical data from other FITNESSGRAM programs. In addition, FG 9 will allow for the import of test scores from other sources such as Excel.

For complete step-by-step instructions, please use the Help files within the program or use the technical data management documents on the FG Web site.

Import Options in FG 8

Use the File pull-down menu located in the program. It is located on the upper-left side of the teacher screen.

The following import options are available:

1. Import from Windows *FITNESSGRAM* 6.0.3 program.
2. Import from Macintosh *FITNESSGRAM* 6.0.1 program.
3. Import from *FITNESSGRAM* 8.0 program.
4. Import from a custom file (school, teacher, class, or student information).
5. Get from your Pocket PC.

Import From Fitnessgram 6: Windows or Mac Programs

If you are using *FITNESSGRAM* 6.0 program and wish to import data into *FITNESSGRAM* 8.0, you will need the latest version of the 6.0. program (6.0.3). The version number is located in the bottom left of the About screen. If you do not have *FITNESSGRAM* 6.0.3, you will need to download the update from the Human Kinetics Web site (www.humankinetics.com) before you can import your 6.0 data into *FITNESSGRAM* 8.0. If you don't do this, your import file will not be processed.

1. Select your import option (choose one):
   a. Windows 6.0.3
   b. Mac 6.0.1
2. Select a creation option for classes and teachers.
3. Select a match option if students are already entered into the program. If so, you need to let the program know if there are duplicate student records in the files and how you want to match them up during the import process (e.g., by name, birthdate, or student ID), or have the program assume that all the student records are new.

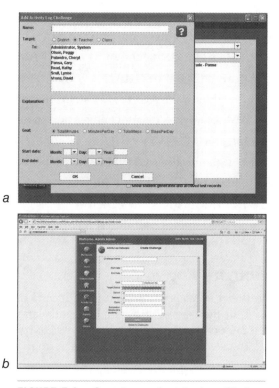

a

b

FIGURE E.9 Creating an Activity Log Challenge in *(a)* FG 8 and *(b)* FG 9.

FIGURE E.10 FG 8 file menu.

4. Use the Browse button to select the location of your files. You can select multiple files to be imported at the same time.

5. Click the Import button.

6. A pop-up box will indicate import progress.

7. An import log will be created if records are not fully imported or if there were errors during the import.

Import From FG 8

1. Make sure you exported using the *FITNESSGRAM* 8.0 format. The import file will be a Zip file.

2. Select the FITNESSGRAM 8.0 import format from the Import menu.

3. Select the Import button when you're ready to import.

4. A pop-up box will indicate import progress.

5. An import log will be created if records are not fully imported.

Custom Import

This option allows you to specify the variables (e.g., student name, grade, gender, date of birth) and the order of the variables. Comma-delimited text or CSV files are required for a custom import. Please see the Help file for complete information on custom imports. Use this import to move current students to new teachers and classes during the school year or at the beginning of the school year.

Export Options in FG 8

Exporting data from *FITNESSGRAM* 8.0 to another version of *FITNESSGRAM* or to another database program is easy. For complete import information and instructions, please refer to the Help file within the program or the *FITNESSGRAM* Web site (www.fitnessgram.net). The following export options are available:

- *FITNESSGRAM* 6.0 export for import into a *FITNESSGRAM* 6.0 program.
- *FITNESSGRAM* 8.0 export for use with the 8.0 program.
- Send to Pocket PC to sync with Pocket PC.
- Research export: The students' names and ID numbers are de-identified so the data cannot be traced to a specific student. Researchers will have access only to district names, school names, state names, and students' data (e.g., gender and grade) and test results.
- State Agency Export that can be used to submit results to a state agency as required or mandated by legislation or state or organization ruling. As of this writing, only California is using this specific export format.
- Achievement of Standards (AOS) Export is located under the Reports menu. Select Export Wizard. The AOS export extracts all test data for each student record in a text file and provides the following information:
  - Relevant student information, including age, grade, gender, and ethnicity
  - Raw score for each test item and if that score is in the Healthy Fitness Zone (Y or N)
  - Score for each test component (e.g., aerobic capacity, body composition) and if that score is in the Healthy Fitness Zone (Y or N)

  With this information, teachers, schools, or districts can compare fitness results with other student information captured by the district, such as academic achievement or student absenteeism.

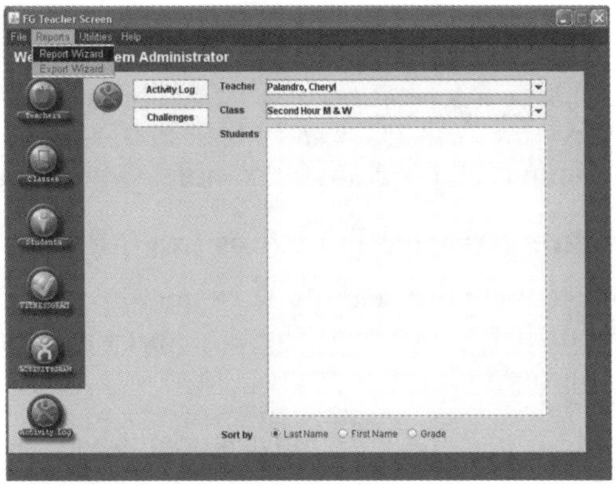

FIGURE E.11   FG 8 Export Wizard.

Import Options in FG 9

The ability to import data relationships, historical data from your FITNESSGRAM 8 program, or FG scores from another source will depend on the permissions set for your program. Following are the import options available in FG 9:

1. Custom import.
   a. Import some or all important data relationships into FG 9, such as district, school, PE teachers, classes, students.
2. Import FG scores from another source such as an Excel file.
3. Import from a PDA device using a specific file format.
4. Import historical data from FITNESSGRAM 8.
   a. When importing from a FG 8 installation, you must make sure that student IDs in FG 8 will match those of FG 9. If not, then student information and previous scores will not merge in FG 9.

Export Options in FG 9

1. Export data.
   a. FG 9 export format provides FG results for each student by raw score for each test item and indicates if the score is in the Healthy Fitness Zone. It also indicates if that score for a fitness component (e.g., body composition, flexibility) is in the Healthy Fitness Zone. This export format is in a csv file and can be used to compare fitness results against other student information captured by a district, such as academic achievement and student absenteeism. Following are some options:
      i. Deidentifying student names and student numbers for privacy concerns
      ii. Keeping student names and student numbers for the data export
   b. FG 8 export format is a zip file. It can be used to send data to another FG 8 installation or to a state agency.
   c. Export data to a csv file format.
   d. Export to a text file compatible with a PDA device.

FIGURE E.12 FG 9 export options.

Administrative Functions

Within FG 8 or FG 9 are several administrative functions involving students, such as promoting students, moving students between classes, teachers, and schools, backup and restore functions, deleting of data, and managing the program.

Basic information is provided here concerning these features for both FG 8 and FG 9. Please review the Help files within each program for complete information.

Administrative Functions in FG 8

Note that your security or permissions level will determine your list of options. These features are located under the Utilities pull-down menu.

1. Move Students: Move students between schools, teachers, and classes.
2. Promote: Promote all students for end-of-year processing.
3. Demote: Reverse the Promote function.

FIGURE E.13 Utilities menu for FG 8.

4. User List: View users currently in the program.

5. Delete Data: Delete selected or All Data options.

6. Backup: Back up data to a specific location.

7. Restore: Restore data if lost.

8. Delete Students by Grade.

9. Delete FITNESSGRAM Tests.

10. Consolidate Data.

11. Default Teacher Password.

12. Advanced Options Password.

13. Delete All Data Password.

Administrative Functions in FG 9

To access these functions in FG 9, click on the Utilities icon. Available in FG 9 under Accounts are the following:

1. Move students to a new class

2. Move students to a new school

3. Activate Users: Activate or deactivate users (students, teachers, or school administrators depending on your permission level).

4. Manage Admin access: Use this feature to grant administrator access (school or district admin security levels) to program users.

FIGURE E.14   Utilities menu for FG 9.

In FITNESSGRAM 9, you can configure or manage your program. Management of FG 9 is to be done at the highest permission level within the program and would typically be accomplished by an IT person or a district administrator. The following are the features included in the program:

1. Required Settings:

   a. Proxy Server.

   b. License Key: This is where a customer manages the purchased site or building licenses for the program.

2. Optional Settings:

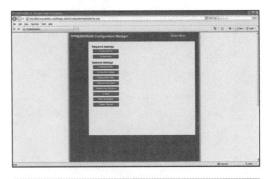

FIGURE E.15   Configuration screen for FG 9.

   a. Ethnicity Codes: Default codes are the federal ethnicity codes. Customers can use these codes or import ethnicity codes specific to the district.

   b. Exemption Codes: If you want to document why a student is not tested (e.g., injury, disability, illness), you can import or enter this information here.

   c. Editing User Data: In this section, you indicate which security or permission levels of teacher, school administrator, or district administrator can add or edit information related to users, including student information.

   d. Editing Class Data: In this section, you indicate which permission levels can add or edit classes or the makeup of those classes (e.g., students and teachers).

   e. Student Permissions: Within the FG 9 program, you can determine if students can access the student application to enter data into FITNESSGRAM, ACTIVITYGRAM, or Activity Log.

   f. E-mail: Indicate if this installation of FG 9 can e-mail FG student and parent reports and forgotten passwords.

   g. Main Navigation: Indicate if any users of FG 9 can have access to ACTIVITYGRAM, Activity Log, or Utilities.

   h. Single Sign-On: Indicate if users of FG 9 will use authenticated single sign-on to access the program.

Student FITNESSGRAM for FG 8 and FG 9

Teachers can use the student *FITNESSGRAM* program to have students enter in their test scores, complete an *ACTIVITYGRAM*, and track their pedometer steps and minutes of activity in the activity log. Use the computer lab in your school, place a computer in the gym, or use a computer in the school library for this purpose.

To log in, each student will need a user name and password. This information was created in the teacher program when students were entered manually or via an import. You can generate a report of students' log-in information. Go to the Reports menu and select the Student Information report.

Note: There are minor differences in the student program for FG 8 and FG 9.

My Info

The first time a student logs into the program, the My Info screen is displayed. It is also accessible via the My Info button at the bottom of the Main Menu screen.

In My Info, students enter or verify several pieces of information, including the following:

- Nickname
- Gender
- Date of birth
- Grade
- User name
- Password
- Ethnicity

Main Menu Screen

At the Main Menu screen, instruct your students to click on either FITNESSGRAM to record test scores and take the physical activity questionnaire, the ACTIVITYGRAM to record their fitness activities over a two- or three-day period, or the Activity Log to record pedometer steps and/or minutes of physical activity.

FITNESSGRAM

Access *FITNESSGRAM* from the Main Menu screen.

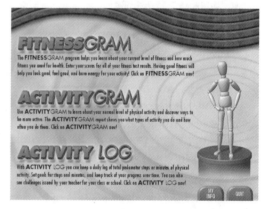

FIGURE E.16   Student log-on screen.

FIGURE E.17   Main menu screen.

FIGURE E.18   My Info screen.

1. To start a new *FITNESSGRAM*, click the new icon. These tests are referred to as student-generated *FITNESSGRAM*s.

2. To view or enter scores in an existing *FITNESSGRAM*, select a *FITNESSGRAM* from the list and click the Open icon. Note that once scores are entered for a teacher-generated *FITNESSGRAM*, students will not be able to edit scores if the test has been locked.

3. To delete a student–generated *FITNESSGRAM*, select the test and click the Delete icon. Students are unable to delete teacher-generated tests.

Entering FITNESSGRAM Test Scores

- Tell your students to follow the on-screen instructions for entering information for each test. (Note: It's best to review the screen and instructions before having your students enter their test scores.)
- To access a specific test, click on the test name or data field and enter the appropriate score in the boxes located at the top of each screen.
- Click the I'm Done button or hit the Enter key after each score is entered. The test score will be displayed with the test.
- **To correct an entry**, click on the test item and re-enter the test score. Click the I'm Done button when completed.
- **To delete an entry**, click on the test item and delete the test score. Make sure to click the I'm Done button.

Physical Activity Questionnaire

In this portion of the student *FITNESSGRAM,* have your students enter the number of days during the last seven days that they participated in aerobic, strength, and flexibility activities.

- Click the Questions button to access the questionnaire.
- Have the students click on the type of activity.
- Read the question at the top of the screen and select the number of days using one of the radio buttons.
- Click the I'm Done button when finished with each activity.
- The number of days spent in an activity will be reflected in the student's *FITNESSGRAM* report.

View or Print a FITNESSGRAM Report

Students view results of their fitness scores via the *FITNESSGRAM* report. This is the same report that is printed from the teacher program. Students should click the View Report button to view their test results. To print the report, students should click the Print Report button. If you have selected to print the *FITNESSGRAM* report in Spanish in the teacher program, the report will also be printed in Spanish from the student program.

ACTIVITYGRAM

In the *ACTIVITYGRAM,* students provide information on their daily activities for a two- or three-day period. This information is then compiled into a report, which provides instant feedback to the students on their daily activity levels. Access *ACTIVITYGRAM* from the Main Menu.

1. Teacher-generated *ACTIVITYGRAM*s will be listed. Highlight the *ACTIVITYGRAM* and click the Open icon. To create a student-generated *ACTIVITYGRAM,* click the New icon.
2. To view or edit an existing *ACTIVITYGRAM,* select the *ACTIVITYGRAM* in the list box and click the Open icon.
3. To delete an *ACTIVITYGRAM,* select it and click the Delete icon.

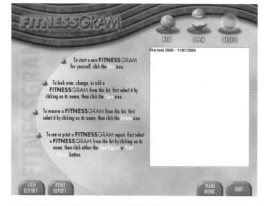

FIGURE E.19   *FITNESSGRAM* menu screen.

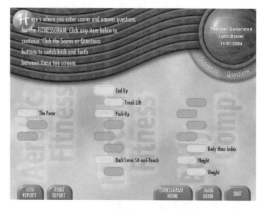

FIGURE E.20   *FITNESSGRAM* scores screen.

FIGURE E.21   Questionnaire screen.

Entering Information

The *ACTIVITYGRAM* screen consists of a grid divided into half-hour segments—from 7:00 AM to 10:30 PM. Students need to enter information for a two- or three-day period. One of these days must be a non-school day. Select either School Day 1, School Day 2, or Non-School Day button at the upper-right of the screen.

- Select the appropriate time by clicking on the half-hour segment. Note that the clock on the right reflects the selected time. Have your students follow the red arrow for the following steps.
- From the activity pyramid at the top left, have your students select an activity category. A submenu of activity options for that category is displayed onscreen.
- Select an activity from the submenu.
- Click on an intensity level for the activity (rest, light, moderate, or vigorous).
- Have the student indicate if the activity was done for some, most, or all of the time for the half-hour segment.
- The last step is to click the I'm Done button to record the entry in the grid.
- Have students complete this sequence for the entire grid to get a complete picture of their activities for that day.

For multiple entries of the same activity over a longer span time, click the I'm Done button as many times as needed.

To correct an entry, click on the time segment and re-enter the information.

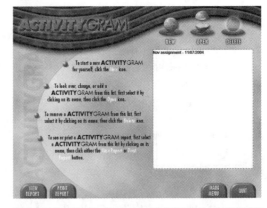

FIGURE E.22   *ACTIVITYGRAM* menu screen.

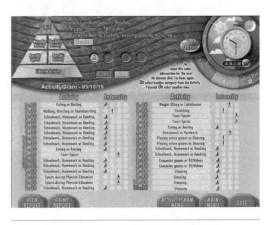

FIGURE E.23   Opened *ACTIVITYGRAM* screen.

View or Print an ACTIVITYGRAM Report

Students view results of their activity entries via the *ACTIVITYGRAM* report. This is the same report that is printed from the teacher program. Students click the View Report button to view their test results. To print the report, students should click the Print Report button.

Activity Log

In the Activity Log, students enter minutes of activity and/or the number of pedometer steps done on a daily basis. Students can also see how their class or school is doing on challenges that may be issued by their teacher to other classes or schools or from other classes and schools issued to their class.

To access the Activity Log, follow these instructions:

1. Click on Activity Log at the Main Menu screen.
2. Students must first enter a goal for steps and/or minutes before entering data. Click OK when done.
3. Pedometer steps is the default option. To change to minutes of activity, click the Minutes button at the top right of the screen. The current month is always displayed on-screen.

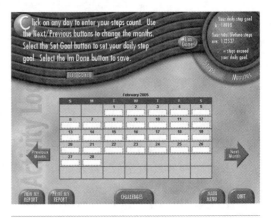

FIGURE E.24   Activity Log.

4. To enter steps or minutes, students need to type the amount in the appropriate day on the calendar.

5. To move back and forth in the calendar, use the back and forward arrows.

6. At the top right, students will be able to see their set goal and the total steps or minutes.

Challenges

To view challenges, students should click the Challenges button at the bottom of the screen, then select a challenge from the list. Students will only see challenges issued from or to their class. They will not see individual results for other students.

Activity Log Report

To print a report, students should click the Print report button, specify a date range, then select the Print button. The report displays the total number of steps and/or minutes of activity and a daily average for the dates selected.

BIBLIOGRAPHY

Note: Readers interested in more documentation related to the *FITNESSGRAM* assessments and the establishment of the Healthy Fitness Zones should consult the *FITNESSGRAM Reference Guide.*

American Alliance for Health, Physical Education, Recreation and Dance. 1996. *Physical Best and Children with Disabilities.* Reston, VA: AAHPERD.

Biddle, S.J.W. 1986. Exercise motivation: Theory and practice. *British Journal of Physical Education* 17: 40-44.

Blair, S.N., Clark, D.G., Cureton, K.J., and Powell, K.E. 1989. Exercise and fitness in childhood: Implications for a lifetime of health. In *Perspectives in Exercise Science and Sports Medicine: Volume 2, Youth Exercise and Sports,* ed. C.V. Gisolfi and D.R. Lamb, pp. 401-430. Indianapolis: Benchmark.

Blair, S.N., Kohl, H.W., Gordon, N.F., and Paffenbarger, R.S. 1992. How much physical activity is good for health? *Annals and Reviews in Public Health* 13: 99-126.

Blair, S.N., Kohl, H.W., Paffenbarger, R.S., Clark, D.G., Cooper, K.H., and Gibbons, L.W. 1989. Physical fitness and all-cause mortality. *Journal of the American Medical Association* 262: 2395-2437.

Caspersen, C.J., Christenson, G.M., and Pollard, R.A. 1986. Status of 1990 physical fitness and exercise objectives—evidence from NHIS 1985. *Public Health Report* 101: 587-592.

Centers for Disease Control and Prevention. 1997. Guidelines for school and community programs to promote lifelong physical activity among young people. *Morbidity and Mortality Weekly Report* 46(RR-6): 1-36.

Corbin, C.B. 1987. Youth fitness, exercise and health: There is much to be done. *Research Quarterly for Exercise and Sport* 58: 308-314.

Corbin, C.B., Lovejoy, P., Steingard, P., and Emerson, R. 1990. Fitness awards: Do they accomplish their intended objectives? *American Journal of Health Promotion* 4: 345-351.

Corbin, C.B., and Pangrazi, R.P. 1998. Physical activity pyramid rebuffs peak experience. *ACSM's Health and Fitness Journal* 2(1): 12-17.

Council for Physical Education for Children. 1998. *Physical Activity for Children: A Statement of Guidelines.* Reston, VA: NASPE.

Dale, D., and Corbin, C.B. 2000. Physical activity participation of high school graduates following exposure to conceptual or traditional physical education. *Research Quarterly for Exercise and Sport* 71(1): 61-68.

Dale, D., Corbin, C.B., and Cuddihy, T.F. 1998. Can conceptual physical education promote physically active lifestyles? *Pediatric Exercise Science* 10(2): 97-109.

Epstein, L.H., Valoski, A., Wing, R.R., and McCurly, J. 1990. Ten-year follow-up of behavioral family-based treatment for obese children. *Journal of the American Medical Association* 264: 2519-2524.

Gortmaker, S.L., Dietz, W.H., Sobol, A.H., and Wehler, C.A. 1987. Increasing pediatric obesity in the U.S. *American Journal of Diseases of Children* 1: 535-540.

Harter, S. 1978. Effectance motivation revisited. *Child Development* 21: 34-64.

Human Kinetics. 1998. *Active Youth: Ideas for Implementing CDC Physical Activity Promotion Guidelines.* Champaign, IL: Human Kinetics.

Johnston, F.W., Hamill, D.V., and Lemeshow, S. 1972. *Skinfold Thickness of Children 6-11 Years, Series 11, No. 120.* Washington, DC: U.S. Center for Health Statistics.

Johnston, F.W., Hamill, D.V., and Lemeshow, S. 1974. *Skinfold Thickness of Children 12-17 Years, Series 11, No. 132.* Washington, DC: U.S. Center for Health Statistics.

Kline, G.M., Porcari, J.P., Hintermeister, R., Freedson, P.S., Ward, A., McCarron, R.F., Ross, J., and Rippe, J.M. 1987. Estimation of $\dot{V}O_2$max from a one-mile track walk, gender, age, and body weight. *Medicine and Science in Sports and Exercise* 19(3): 253-259.

Krahenbuhl, G.S., Skinner, J.S., and Kohrt, W.M. 1985. Developmental aspects of maximal aerobic power in children. *Exercise and Sport Sciences Reviews* 13: 503-538.

Leger, L., and Lambert, J. 1982. A maximal 20-m shuttle run test to predict $\dot{V}O_2$max. *European Journal of Applied Physiology* 49: 1-12.

Leger, L.A., Mercier, D., Gadoury, C., and Lambert, J. 1988. The multistage 20 metre shuttle run test for aerobic fitness. *Journal of Sport Sciences* 6: 93-101.

Locke, E.A., and Lathan, G.P. 1985. The application of goal setting to sports. *Journal of Sport Psychology* 7: 205-222.

Lohman, T.G. 1987. The use of skinfold to estimate body fatness in children and youth. *Journal of Physical Education, Recreation and Dance* 58(9): 98-102.

Lohman, T.G. 1992. *Advances in Body Composition.* Champaign, IL: Human Kinetics.

Malina, R.M. 1996. Tracking of physical activity and physical fitness across the lifespan. *Research Quarterly for Exercise and Sport* 67(3): 48-57.

Massicote, D. 1990. *Project # 240-0010-88/89: Partial Curl-Up, Push-Ups, and Multistage 20 Meter Shuttle Run, National Norms for 6 to 17 Year-Olds.* Montreal, Canada: Canadian Association for Health, Physical Education and Recreation and Fitness and Amateur Sport Canada.

McSwegin, P.J., Plowman, S.A., Wolff, G.M., and Guttenberg, G.L. 1998. The validity of a one-mile walk test for high school age individuals. *Measurement in Physical Education and Exercise Science* 2(1): 47-63.

Pangrazi, R.P., Corbin, C.B., and Welk, G.J. 1996. Physical activity for children and youth. *Journal of Physical Education, Recreation and Dance* 67(4): 38-43.

Pate, R.R., Baranowski, T., Dowda, M., and Trost, S.G. 1996. Tracking of physical activity in young children. *Medicine and Science in Sports and Exercise* 28(1): 92-96.

Pate, R.R., and Hohn, R.C. 1994. A contemporary mission for physical education. In *Health and Fitness Through Physical Education,* ed. R.R. Pate and R.C. Hohn, pp. 1-8. Champaign, IL: Human Kinetics.

Pate, R.R., Ross, J.G., Dotson, C., and Gilbert, G.G. 1985. The new norms: A comparison with the 1980 AAHPERD norms. *Journal of Physical Education, Recreation and Dance* 56(1): 28-30.

Ross, J.G., Pate, R.R., Lohman, T.G., and Christenson, G.M. 1987. Changes in the body composition of children. *Journal of Physical Education, Recreation and Dance* 58(9): 74-77.

Sallis, J.F., and Patrick, K. 1994. Physical activity guidelines for adolescents: Consensus statement. *Pediatric Exercise Science* 6: 302-314.

Schiemer, S. 1996. The pacer—a really fun run. In *Ideas for Action II: More Award Winning Approaches to Physical Activity.* Reston, VA: AAHPERD.

Slaughter, M.H., Lohman, T.G., Boileau, R.A., Horswill, C.A., Stillman, R.J., Van Loan, M.D., and Benben, D.A. 1988. Skinfold equations for estimation of body fatness in children and youth. *Human Biology* 60: 709-723.

Troiano, R.P., and Flegal, K.M. 1998. Overweight children and adolescents: Description, epidemiology, and demographics. *Pediatrics* 101(3): 497-504.

Troiano, R.P., Flegal, K.M., Kuczmarski, R.J., Campbell, S.M., and Johnson, C.L. 1995. Overweight prevalence and trends for children and adolescents. *Archives of Pediatric and Adolescent Medicine* 149: 1085-1091.

U.S. Department of Health and Human Services. 1996. *Physical Activity and Health: A Report of the Surgeon General.* Atlanta: U.S. Department of Health and Human Services, Centers for Disease Control and Prevention, and National Center for Chronic Disease Prevention and Health Promotion.

Welk, G.J. 1999. The youth physical activity promotion model: A conceptual bridge between theory and practice. *Quest* 51: 5-23.

Weston, A.T., Petosa, R., and Pate, R.R. 1997. Validation of an instrument for measurement of physical activity in youth. *Medicine and Science in Sports and Exercise* 29(1): 138-143.

Whitehead, J.R., and Corbin, C.B. 1991. Youth fitness testing: The effects of percentile-based evaluative feedback on intrinsic motivation. *Research Quarterly for Exercise and Sport* 62: 225-231.

Williams, D.P., Going, S.B., Lohman, T.G., Harsha, D.W., Webber, L.S., and Bereson, G.S. 1992. Body fatness and the risk of elevated blood pressure, total cholesterol and serum lipoprotein ratios in children and youth. *American Journal of Public Health* 82: 358-363.

Winnick, J.P., and Short, F.X. 1985. *Physical Fitness Testing of the Disabled: Project Unique.* Champaign, IL: Human Kinetics.

Winnick, J.P., and Short, F.X. 1999. *The Brockport Physical Fitness Test Manual.* Champaign, IL: Human Kinetics.

Winnick, J.P., and Short, F.X. 1999. *The Brockport Physical Fitness Training Guide.* Champaign, IL: Human Kinetics.

ABOUT THE EDITORS

Marilu Dooley Meredith

Gregory J. Welk

Marilu Dooley Meredith, EdD, is the director of the Perot International Data Center at The Cooper Institute. She previously served as the national program director for *FITNESSGRAM*. Before joining the staff at The Cooper Institute, Meredith worked as a physical educator in a suburban community. She has been an integral member of the *FITNESSGRAM* staff since the program began in 1982.

   Gregory J. Welk, PhD, is an assistant professor in the department of health and human performance at Iowa State University, where he teaches health promotion–related courses and conducts research on the assessment and promotion of physical activity. He previously worked for The Cooper Institute for Aerobics Research in Dallas, Texas, where he served as the director of childhood and adolescent health and the scientific director of the *FITNESSGRAM* youth fitness program. He continues to serve as the scientific director of the program and focuses much of his research on testing and improving the application of *FITNESSGRAM* and *ACTIVITYGRAM* assessments.

About The Cooper Institute

Founded in 1970 by Kenneth H. Cooper, MD, MPH, The Cooper Institute is a nonprofit research and education center dedicated to advancing the understanding of the relationship between living habits and health, and to providing leadership in implementing these concepts to enhance people's physical and emotional well-being.

FitnessGram®

IN PARTNERSHIP WITH

NFL Play 60

THE NFL MOVEMENT FOR AN ACTIVE GENERATION

Web-based Fitnessgram 10 now available!

The Web-based Fitnessgram 10 offers a host of new benefits for school systems of all sizes:

- Web-based data collection means that no client installations are required, saving tech installation and support time.

- Teachers can access data from anywhere that has an Internet connection (when the district has set permissions to allow this).

- Teachers can save time and paper and ensure students' privacy by e-mailing Fitnessgram reports to students and parents.

- Expanded options for generating statistical reports, including reader-friendly graphics, make Fitnessgram reports more meaningful.

- Districts can mandate test items, eliminating confusion and standardizing test items districtwide.

- Teachers can quickly and easily import test scores from other sources.

- Teachers can identify and record students who are exempt from taking one or more test items due to disability or injury.

- Tech staff can import relevant student information along with teacher and class relationships to quickly get teachers ready to enter scores. .

- Enterprise or web-hosted versions available for schools, districts, and states.

For more information

visit **www.Fitnessgram.net**

or contact your Human Kinetics K-12 sales rep at k12sales@hkusa.com or 800-747-4457.

HUMAN KINETICS
The Information Leader in Physical Activity & Health
Publisher of Fitnessgram®

Fitnessgram® is developed and owned by

The Cooper Institute

2335   8/13